C000146677

IGNITE YOUR
CHURCH

IGNITE YOUR
CHURCH

Seven Practices to Be an Architect and Not an Arsonist

Troy H. Jones

with Josh Kelley

Copyright © 2021 by Troy H. Jones

All rights reserved. No part of this publication may be reproduced, stored in a retrieval system, or transmitted in any form or by any means—electronic, mechanical, photocopy, recording, or otherwise—except for brief quotations in printed reviews, without the prior written permission of the publisher.

ISBN:

Hardcover:	978-1-954024-10-6
Paperback:	978-1-954024-11-3
Ebook:	978-1-954024-12-0

Unless otherwise noted, passages of Scripture are from THE HOLY BIBLE, NEW INTERNATIONAL VERSION®, NIV® Copyright © 1973, 1978, 1984, 2011 by Biblica, Inc.® Used by permission. All rights reserved worldwide.

To all the pillars and senior adults of New Life Church:

The patience and grace you have demonstrated
all these years blows me away.

Thank you for believing in our *mission* more than our *methods*.

CONTENTS

Introduction 1

1   The Igniter.. 11

Section I

The Seven Practices

2   Practice #1: Confront the Status Quo......................... 21

3   Practice #2: Clarify Your Culture............................... 31

4   Practice #3: Trust the Story 47

5   Practice #4: Triage Changes...................................... 59

6   Practice #5: Dance, Don't Fight! 77

7   Practice #6: Reset the Beams 89

8   Practice #7: Make it Stick!....................................... 103

Section II

The MCI

9   The MCI Relaunch Plan 119

10   Define It What is "It"? 129

11   Date It: When Will You Do "It"? 141

12   Do It: How Will You Do "It"? 153

13   A Culture of Change 163

      About Troy H. Jones 171

      Resources 172

      Endorsements 174

FOREWORD

by Rob Ketterling

I'm not good at home improvement—I don't even hang curtain rods or picture frames! I'm always going to call an expert. When they show up and handle the project with ease, I wonder why I hired them but then realize they've done this many times before and know the shortcuts, the pitfalls, and the tricks of the trade. I'm grateful for their skills that fix my problems—and save my marriage!

There are experts in every area of life. Most of us don't have the time, skillset, or insider's knowledge to become an expert, but the problem is that we can't muster up the courage to make the call for help. If we really look at what they save us—time, frustration, sub-par results—the experts are worth every dollar. Everyone wins when they use their gifts to save the day.

If you have this book in your hands, you're making the call! It doesn't mean you're a bad pastor; it means you have the courage to ask for help to become the leader God has called you to be.

In *Ignite Your Church*, my friend Troy Jones has answered your call, and he's a true expert. Watch him work as he gives you step-by-step plans to make your church the church you dreamed it could be! You'll be inspired by his stories, encouraged by his insight, and strengthened for the work ahead. *Ignite Your Church* is more than an inspiring read—his "MCI Relaunch Strategy" is a proven way to recalibrate your church.

I'm excited for you and—I have to admit—I'm excited for me as I also get to apply the tools and the insights this book has to offer. Our church isn't old, but we need a tune-up and re-calibration to go to the next level. You can trust Troy's plan. Dig into this book, put in the hard work, and get ready for the future you want for your church and ministry!

Rob Ketterling

Lead Pastor, River Valley Church
and Author of *Speed of Unity*

INTRODUCTION

This is my house. Built in 1896 on land that was part of a homestead grant (signed by President Ulysses S. Grant), it used to be known as the "Mercer House" because it had been owned by one of Seattle's founders. It didn't look this good when Jana and I moved  in. Not even close. Leaking roof. Trash everywhere. Outdated plumbing and tube wiring. Orange countertops. Old house smell wafting off furniture from who knows where.

When Jana first saw it, she said, "There's no way we'll *ever* live in this place!"

"But, honey," I said, "it has character! It's full of history."

In 1979, Renton Assembly (now New Life Church) purchased the property of 57.37 acres and this one worn-out house for its future campus. They had planned to demolish it, but it spent the next decade being used as a homeless shelter, a home for missionaries on furlough, short-term housing for interns, and now a parsonage for their new youth pastor—me—and his young wife.

I hated the thought of "this old house" being destroyed. It was filled with potential and had so much history. Hanging out in the living room and playing Monopoly with some good friends (I'm a Monopoly fanatic—I don't know what that says about me), I was moving one of those plastic green

1

houses to a new property and jokingly said, "You know, we could just move this house. Somebody has to save it."

"I bet you could," said one of my friends. "Go for it!"

Twenty-eight years old, no experience with historical houses…challenge accepted!

Six months later, at 4:00 a.m. on June 3rd, 1995, the 70-ton Mercer House began a four-hour and two-mile trip down the Renton-Maple Valley highway. Jana had the honor of hitting the lever for the special hydraulic system that evenly lifted the house to protect the rigid lath-and-plaster interior walls. With the move complete and the house in place, the real work began. We had to build a new foundation, install a new roof and kitchen, strip some of the interior walls down to studs, and bring the wiring and plumbing up to code. It took several years and was completed in several phases, but in the end, we had a practically new house, without losing any of the original charm and character.

Would it have been easier to buy a brand-new house? Absolutely! Probably a little cheaper, too. But now we have a house that has genuine character and craftsmanship that you can't find in other houses. Wood floors. Tall ceilings. Beautiful balconies and pitched roofs. Scallop siding. Unique staircase. Contractors have told me that you can't even buy wood and nails of this quality today. More importantly, this is our *home*. This is where we raised our daughters and play with our grandchildren.

We wouldn't trade it for all the "new house smell" in the world.

Restorationists

Did you know there are architects that specialize in historic buildings? In the 18th and 19th centuries, the "architectural conservation movement" gained momentum in response to modernism. In contrast to a culture that believes "Newer is better!" these architects see old buildings as treasures to be protected.

Within the movement, there are two schools of thought: The Preservationist believes old buildings shouldn't be changed; they're fine the way they are and only need to be preserved. The Restorationist wants to preserve the character of old buildings while improving them with modern materials and techniques. Restoration is a completely different game from "merely" preserving an old building or designing a new one from scratch. There's an art to bringing a historic building up to code and making it functional in the modern world while preserving its character and beauty. It requires more than skill, it requires a special kind of passion.

When it comes to both houses and the established church—churches that have been around for decades—I'm a Restorationist. I love churches with a rich history, even if they are stuck in tradition, crippled by endless leadership transitions, and just can't move forward. Many others have given up on established churches, saying they have one foot in the grave and should just be shut down. Church-growth seminars and even whole denominations are more interested in planting brand-new churches than restoring old churches.

I don't buy it. Not even close.

These beautiful churches have seen the effects of wars, economic upheaval and prosperity, demographic changes, and sweeping cultural movements. They have stability and potential that no new church plant will ever have. They are like my old house—filled with stories from before my time and built with greater craftsmanship than any of the new builds that have taken over the hills of my hometown.

Also like my old house, they need someone to put sweat equity into them. They need someone to see beyond the outdated features and bring back their former glory. Not preserved as a historical monument, but restored to be vibrant and effective churches in their community and throughout the world. If you're adventurous enough to recapture and restore the beauty of your established church, it will be well worth every ounce of time and energy. In fact, I believe that the greatest potential for reaching America lies in waking up our countless established churches and helping them recapture their purpose.

Are you ready to bring your church back to life?

What Makes This Book Different

In 2014, I founded "The Recalibrate Group," a coaching service dedicated to helping pastors renovate and ignite their churches. I'm drawn to the term recalibrate because it means "returning to the original settings and specifications." Recalibrating a church means "restoring its mission and heartbeat." It means lighting a fire in the heart of the pastor, Leadership Community (i.e., the entirety of your leadership team, including staff and oversight board), church, and everyone who is part of the congregation. Recalibration and restoration. Those are two of my favorite metaphors (and I'm a "metaphor guy") for the one concept that's at the heart of this book— returning churches to their original mission, but within their modern context.

It's not a matter of "if" but "when" a church will need to be recalibrated/restored—just like it's only a question of when my house will need a new roof. All churches naturally become ingrown over time. They become about taking care of Christians instead of discipling people. About making insiders happy instead of reaching outsiders. About paying the bills instead of having a kingdom impact. About protecting outdated ministries instead of developing new ideas that serve the lost.

Because all churches drift, this book is for any and every leader who wants to either ignite a fire under their church or keep the fire lit. I've been in ministry for thirty years and spent the last seventeen years leading New Life, a church with an incredible foundation of nearly a hundred years but that was in desperate need of major renovation. I've paid the price and made all the mistakes. I've also coached countless pastors of established churches and seen the good, bad, and ugly of leading God's flock.

Over that time, I discovered and developed the MCI Relaunch Strategy—a revolutionary and practical technique that can change everything. A match that lights the fire. But fire is dangerous stuff. It can excite and energize a congregation or destroy, in one hour, a church that took one hundred years to build. After getting burned more than once, I've also developed seven hard-won practices you'll want to master before striking that match.

These principles and tools apply regardless of the age of your church and you don't necessarily need to be the lead pastor to implement them. But this book is uniquely focused on established churches because they aren't typically addressed in church-growth books or at leadership seminars. Leaders like Rick Warren, Andy Stanley, Craig Groeschel, and Steven Furtick are all great men who made great contributions to the Church (and have enriched my life), but they *planted* their churches. They haven't experienced the challenges you face pastoring a church with decades of history. Remodeling a house and building a new one may look similar to outsiders, but any architect will tell you that they take radically different skills, and this book focuses on *those* skills.

Another thing I think makes this book different is that I focus on recalibration, not revitalization. Here's what I mean. Revitalization is for churches that are barely alive (even if people don't want to admit it). One of the fundamental problems in church leadership is that we focus on churches that need revitalization and all but ignore churches that are what I would call deceptively healthy. One is barely alive; the other is alive but ineffective. One can barely pay their bills; the other is paying their bills but not reaching people with the gospel.

Recalibrating is a normal part of keeping a car running smoothly; the best way to prevent breakdowns is regular maintenance. The best way to keep your church from dying is to continually and systematically recalibrate—to return her to her mission.

Things to Know About Me

First, I'm a pastor, not someone writing from an ivory tower or in an academic setting. While I'm very much a "systems guy"—I dream in graphs and am wired to find patterns, solutions, and strategies—the ideas in this book have been forged on the anvil of personal experience and by coaching hundreds of pastors. I practice what I preach and use these principles in every aspect of my life.

Second, I'm committed to the local church because it changed my life. I was raised in a broken home and am the first Christian in my family. My oldest brother spent thirteen years in prison, the middle one was on drugs and died a couple of years ago, and my youngest brother is living on the streets because of mental illness. But the people at a local church loved me, sent their bus to my house every Sunday, and paid for me to go to a Bible camp in the summer of 1980—$55 that I can never fully pay back! I will do anything and everything to help church leaders do today what that church did for me yesterday. If God hadn't used those people to care for me, I'd likely be divorced, living on the street, in prison, or even dead. By the way, the name of that local church is New Life. Yes, I'm pastoring the very church that sent a bus to my house. My life was saved and transformed by a local church, so I'm very much biased towards her.

> **PRO TIP |**
> Trying to recalibrate without love is like throwing a Molotov cocktail. If you struggle with genuinely loving (and liking) your church, start a "What I love about my church" journal and set a reminder on your phone to add a new entry each day.

Third, I'm deeply committed to the Great Commission—to develop fully devoted followers of Jesus—and compelled by the unconditional love of Christ. At the end of the day, Christianity boils down to loving God and loving one another. If you're motivated by numbers, fame, or finances, this book will be a waste of time. The unconditional covenant love of Jesus Christ must be our motivation and source of strength.

And fourth, I'm convinced you can do this. You can ignite a fire in your church without being an arsonist. I know you can because I've seen many other church leaders, just like you, do it. God is already working in and through you. I promise to be practical and not waste your time with a bunch of theories that won't work. I just want to come alongside and give you the scaffolding for building higher, to the glory of God and for the sake of His church.

Where We're Going

A few years ago, I wrote a book called *Recalibrate Your Church* based on my doctoral thesis. Since then, I've coached over 400 pastors through its principles; this book is a result of walking alongside pastors from churches of every size, denomination, and culture. It has gone from a thesis to a practical instruction manual.

Here's the game plan:

In the next chapter, I'll introduce you to the Recalibrate Ignitor, or what I call the Mission Critical Initiative (MCI). It is, without a doubt, the single most powerful tool I've discovered for lighting a fire under your church. It's your igniter, your match, your one thing that changes everything. It will galvanize you and your Leadership Community and recalibrate your church.

In Section 1 (chapters 2-8), I'll teach you seven vital practices that will both fuel the fire and equip you to be an architect and not an arsonist. Without these practices, that match will be, at best, a firework that goes off in a flash and is nothing more than a lot of noise. At worst, it will torch your entire church.

In Section 2 (chapters 9-13), I'll bring it all together with a very practical and attainable MCI Relaunch Plan: "Define it. Date it. Do it."

Along the way, I'll sprinkle in some "Pro Tips" and stories of pastors who've been where you are.

Finally—and this is really important—at the end of each chapter, you'll find the "Recalibrate NOW" sections. The "Think About it!" questions are designed to help you assimilate what you've read. The "Talk About it!" questions will be most effective if you discuss them with trusted members of your team.

Lastly, the "Take action!" is a single practical activity to help you recalibrate the heart and soul of your church. It's the "secret sauce" of this book. Every time I coach a church through a recalibration, I have them create a Strategy Booklet and MCI Relaunch Plan (I'll explain these in time). If you faithfully complete the exercises, you'll effectively create your own Strategy Booklet and MCI Relaunch Plan, giving you a blueprint to recalibrate your church. As a bonus, you can download a customizable template for both at: www.recalibrategroup.com/strategybooklet.

PRO TIP |
Recalibrating is not a "Lone Ranger" job. Find two to three trusted people to journey with you and buy them copies of this book, then schedule a regular date to discuss the "Talk About It!" questions. (Bulk discounts at: www.recalibrategroup.com/ igniteyourchurch.)

In the same way that New Life had to choose between demolishing the Mercer House or letting their crazy youth pastor move it down the street and restore it, you have two options: become a restoration architect and restore your church's former glory, or be an arsonist and burn it down. I pray you will join me and become a skillful architect—let's rediscover the beauty of this old house!

RECALIBRATE NOW

Introduction: Check Your Readiness

THINK ABOUT IT!

1. Summarize the big idea of this chapter in your own words.
2. What is something new you learned?
3. What is something you disagree with or don't understand?

TALK ABOUT IT!

1. Why did you buy this book?
2. What do you hope to get out of it?
3. What do you love about your church?
4. How are the words "recalibrate" and "renovate" similar? How are they different?

TAKE ACTION!

Recalibrating isn't for the faint of heart. Set aside one morning this week to check your own readiness:

- ☐ **Soul:** Are you connected to God and depending on His Spirit?
- ☐ **Relationships:** Are you in a healthy place with your family?
- ☐ **Pastoral heart:** Will love be your motivation?
- ☐ **Health:** Are you taking care of yourself?
- ☐ **Commitment:** Will you be at this church long enough to make change stick?

1

THE IGNITER

"One thing can change everything."

— *Recalibrate Axiom*

A few years ago, I was asked to speak at a denominational conference. One of the leaders, a friend of mine, spoke the first night. He cast his vision for the denomination to the pastors and gave them a long list of goals. After his message, he asked me, "How did I do?"

"I'm going to shoot straight," I said. "The pastors like you. They respect you, so whatever you say is fine with them. But the problem is you gave them so many goals that you effectively gave them no goals. They'll dabble in all of them, but they won't do anything significant."

He looked stunned, but I could see his wheels spinning. The next morning he asked me, "Okay, so what should I have told them?"

"You need to determine the *one* thing that changes everything. The one single, clear, compelling initiative that makes everyone shout, 'Game on!' The one thing that will ignite a new fire and passion in your pastors. The one thing that gets the people back on mission and restores the beauty of their church."

Here's the truth about leading people:

- A big vision doesn't move people if it's too vague.
- A long list of goals puts people to sleep or overwhelms them.
- Personal charisma wins affirmation, but it doesn't change lives.
- Even the best ideas don't change anything unless they are put into action.

- Simply being a faithful and godly leader won't cause transformational change in your church.

- All the vision in the world won't light a fire if there is no clear, compelling, and *timebound* "initiative" with it.

Your people can't focus on ten things. I'm not patronizing them—you and I can't either. They can only focus on one thing. One igniter that will light a fire. This is my igniter, my Recalibrate Strategy that can change everything: the Mission Critical Initiative. Not a list of ten goals that impresses people but fails to bring lasting change, but a bold initiative that creates momentum and unites your church to make the greatest impact. For a season, it's the *one* vision, *one* rallying cry, and *one* challenge that brings everyone together and becomes what Malcolm Gladwell calls a "tipping point."

Pay attention to the words: "Mission"—the mission of God, the very purpose for your church's existence. "Critical"—can't wait, must happen now, the mission may fail without it. And "Initiative"—a single project or event that initiates change. This isn't about tinkering with your church, but relaunching it. In fact, I believe in relaunching a church every three to five years and launching or relaunching specific ministries annually.

Did you just choke on your coffee? This is what our rapidly changing culture requires—if you don't relaunch your church that often, you'll become irrelevant and ineffective. Yes, it's audacious, but it works. I've led my church through four relaunches, not to mention the one we now have on deck (and the countless ministries that New Life has launched or relaunched), and I've coached over 300 churches through their own relaunch. We've got this.

Or maybe you rolled your eyes instead—another gimmick with banners and flyers, excitement with little substance. And if done wrong, it would be. That's what makes the seven practices of Section 1 vital. They'll help you anchor the MCI in transformational change.

In short, this is how it works:

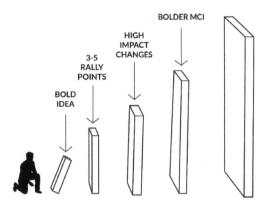

A pastor, on his or her knees, discovers and implements a Bold Idea that's designed to galvanize the church and produce *three to five Rally Points* and a series of *High Impact Changes*. But don't stop there! Harness this momentum for another, *bolder MCI*.

The Power of Momentum

We're all familiar (more or less) with Newton's laws of motion. The first law of motion: Objects at rest tend to stay at rest unless acted upon by an outside force. Imagine a long line of dominos lined up and branching off in multiple streams sweeping around a large auditorium, all waiting for that first domino to fall. Like your church, those dominos represent a massive amount of potential energy but, as Mr. Newton tells us, they're going to "remain at rest" until an outside force gets them moving.

A Mission Critical Initiative is that first domino, the outside force that starts this chain reaction. Here is an important point I don't want you to miss: Thanks to all that potential energy, the first domino can unleash a cascade of change that is vastly disproportionate to its size. Physicist Lorne Whitehead discovered that a domino can knock down another that's fifty percent larger than itself. Using the power of momentum, a chain reaction of twenty-nine dominos of increasing size could theoretically topple the Empire State Building.

Now that's momentum!

If I had just one minute to coach every pastor of every established church, I'd give them this piece of advice: Stop trying to change everything and focus on the ONE domino that will have the greatest impact on your church. Don't worry about all the other problems. Discover the one thing that can ignite a flame of passion in the hearts of your people. That is what an MCI is.

Without momentum, a church at rest will stay at rest. Therefore, the job of the leader is to strategically direct momentum, so it unlocks your church's potential energy and upsets the status quo, which in turn creates more momentum.

Mission-Critical Questions

So how do you find the right domino, your igniter, your one thing?

You *don't* start by asking "What's most important?" I'm serious. Instead, the authors of *The 4 Disciplines of Execution* say, "begin by asking 'If every other area of our operation remained at its current level of performance, what is the one area where change would have the greatest impact?'"[1] That's the question: What will make the biggest impact now?

A couple of years ago, I was talking to a friend whose church had been around since the parting of the Red Sea. Like so many established churches, it had a powerful story but was stuck. He'd been to all the seminars and read all the books, without success, and had become a little cynical.

I tried to explain to him the power of asking what will make the biggest difference.

"It sounds like you're just saying I need to figure out what's most important, right? Been there, done that."

"Not quite," I responded. "You can list many important things, but only one is mission critical right now. We're not creating a list of priorities. We're identifying one initiative that is so audacious that it ignites a fire in your church."

I watched his mind shift into gear and his cynicism evaporate.

---

[1] Chris McChesney, Sean Covey, and Jim Huling, *The 4 Disciplines of Execution* (New York: Free Press, 2012), p. 32.

"I get it! One thing that makes people's eyes light up. Makes them say, 'I see it! Count me in!'"

It's easy to be paralyzed by the future. We focus on dominos three, five, or ten years away and get nothing done today. But today's momentum is the only way to take down tomorrow's dominos. Your job is to identify the one initiative that energizes your church to pray again, dream again, stretch their faith again, and engage their emotional and spiritual muscles. That's the domino that will recalibrate their passion for God and for the lost.

Are you starting to feel overwhelmed? Don't! I'm going to lead you each step of the way and, by the time you finish this book, you'll have your own God-given MCI.

Or maybe you're thinking, "I've got this. Let's go knock down some dominos and start a bonfire. God help the board member who gets in my way!" Hang on a moment. Just like moving my house two miles down the road, there are right and wrong ways to renovate. This requires the skill of an architect, not the impulsiveness of a pyromaniac. Do it wrong and you just might watch your established church become charred ruins. As I said in the introduction, there are seven practices you'll need to honor your congregation and the church's heritage, even as you recalibrate it.

> **PRO TIP |**
> Set a "placeholder" launch date for your MCI and write it in the margin right now. Tell your spouse or a trusted friend. That's right. Set a date for your MCI before you fully understand what it is or how it works. Instant motivation and accountability!

Your Moonshot

On May 25th, 1961, President Kennedy committed the United States of America to what was, at the time, an almost unbelievable goal. "I believe that this nation should commit itself to achieving the goal, before this decade is out, of landing a man on the moon and returning him safely to Earth."

Think of this as an incredibly well-crafted MCI: The president declared a bold initiative and set a date. The nation was captivated by this leader, his speech, and the audacity of his goal. Over the next seven years, 400,000 people dedicated their talents and hearts to the program. Some even gave their lives. Around every corner was a new roadblock, another reason to give up. Each one was met with resolve, tenacity, and passion. On July 21st, 1969, when Neil Armstrong said, "That's one small step for man, one giant leap for mankind," he was speaking on behalf of the entire nation.

This one domino caused a cascade of changes: NASA engineers perfected the fly-by-wire control system still used by airlines and most cars. Pillsbury was enlisted to provide microbe-free food and those techniques now protect us from food-borne illnesses in meat, poultry, and many other food products. The protective space suits yielded a fabric now used by firefighters. The bone-rattling rockets required new shock absorbers, which are now used on bridges and buildings, especially in quake-prone areas. Batteries used on the Apollo missions have been adapted for hearing aids and wireless earbuds. NASA has listed over 2,000 spinoff products that are a direct result of the engineering marvels that put men on the moon. On that eventful day in 1961, I doubt President Kennedy was thinking of keeping chicken fresh or designing earbuds. The domino effect always extends far beyond the original vision.

President Kennedy's MCI is where we got the expression "moonshot." An extremely ambitious project to achieve a monumental goal. Your MCI is your moonshot, your bold move, your match to light a fire in your church. It is your chance to say, "God has done amazing things here, but our best days are still ahead!"

Are you ready for it? Is God stirring your vision? Are you ready for your moonshot?

Let's do this!

RECALIBRATE PROFILE: STAN RUSSELL
Horizon Community Church, (Tualatin, OR)
Part 1

In 2013, our church had just completed a fundraising campaign and built a new building. It wasn't exactly great timing because the country was coming out of the Great Recession. We thought the new building would give us a huge boost, but our giving went *down* 25% and our attendance dropped from 1,000 to 700. I told God, "I don't know how to do this. I need your help."

I fasted and prayed. I poured out my heart to Him. I walked around our church's forty acres each day for six days and seven times on the seventh. It didn't matter. I'd lost confidence and my courage had evaporated.

A few days later, I was in Seattle with Troy and Jana Jones. I told Troy what was happening at our church, and God gave him a message just for me. Realizing that I only needed to focus on one initiative helped me move from stagnation to momentum. We planned to relaunch our church with a Mission Critical Initiative called "Horizon 2.0." We set a date, identified some big Rally Points and High Impact Changes, and prepared for six months. On Launch Day, 325 new people showed up at church! After eight weeks, our attendance was up twenty percent . . . and stayed up. More importantly, we gained something we hadn't had for a long time: momentum.

If you have any doubts that this book will help you—don't. These principles work. You will create momentum in ways you never thought possible.

RECALIBRATE NOW

Chapter 1: Read This with Your Leadership Community

THINK ABOUT IT!

1. Summarize the big idea of this chapter in your own words.

2. What is something new you learned?

3. What is something you disagree with or don't understand?

TALK ABOUT IT!

1. Why shouldn't you ask, "What's the most important thing for my church to do?"

2. How would you describe a Mission Critical Initiative?

3. What do dominos teach you about momentum?

TAKE ACTION!

Order a case of books and read this together with your pastoral team and perhaps a few other key leaders. Is this a big investment of time and energy? Absolutely. But, as we'll talk about in Chapter 6, change of this magnitude requires complete buy-in from your team. Read the chapters and gather to complete the "Recalibrate NOW" sections together. Make these discussions a high priority.

Section I
THE SEVEN PRACTICES

"Be an architect, not an arsonist."

—*Recalibrate Axiom*

2

CONFRONT THE STATUS QUO

"Leaders disrupt the status quo."

—Recalibrate Axiom

Have you ever visited someone's house and been invited to sit on a couch that had an unusual "scent," and you used the "I sit at a desk all day and it feels good to stand" excuse? The smell was obvious to you but not to them. Or maybe you've come back from a vacation and wondered, "Is this what visitors smell?" But in less than an hour, your home smells normal again. It's amazing how quickly people experience "nose blindness" in their own homes.

The same thing happens at your church. Given enough time, we stop seeing things that are painfully clear to others. Sometimes, we even have a vested interest in not noticing because it will mean acknowledging our own shortcomings. Whatever the cause, blindness keeps us stuck, which is why leaders can't ever settle in—it's their job to disrupt the status quo.

Do you wonder if you've been tolerating the status quo and have stopped "smelling the couch"? The answer is "Yes, you probably have!" All of us get used to our environment and we need fresh eyes. Moses needed Jethro. The early church needed Paul the apostle. Whether it's a coach, consultant, mentor, or even a trusted friend, we need someone to give us a fresh perspective on our church. Listening to outside voices has become how we do things at New Life, and that's been key to confronting the status quo. That to say, we need a large, economy-size bottle of holy discontent. "Holy"

21

meaning that this isn't being in a bad mood because attendance is down—it's the unsettled feeling that comes from falling short of God's mission. That's what drives us past the comfort of self-deception and on to a zeal for doing whatever it takes to fulfill His mission.

> **PRO TIP |**
> Churches have no problem giving an honorarium to a guest preacher. Why not invest some of that money into hiring a consultant as a fresh pair of eyes? The long-term benefits will be greater than any single sermon could provide. Better yet, add "professional coaching and consultation services" into your budget.

Time to Galvanize!

There's a reason "Confront the Status Quo" is the first of the seven practices—unless you can courageously do this, your Mission Critical Initiative will never, ever get off the ground. I promise you that.

Why?

Because changing the culture of a church is hard, hard work. Unless you, your leadership, and your church can clearly see how badly you need to recalibrate, you won't be able to overcome the inertia of staying the same. Said another way, the purpose of this practice is to *galvanize* your entire Leadership Community and entire church family. To galvanize means to shock into taking action and strengthen for the task.

Here's the thing. You can't discover and execute your MCI by yourself. You must get buy-in from the team. You must rally them together for your moonshot. To get your leadership on board with the solution, they first have to see the problem. Done right, confronting the status quo will galvanize the entire Leadership Community, so they can then help create excitement in the church for your bold MCI.

Say It Out Loud

In the last "Recalibrate Profile," Pastor Stan Russell talked about how Horizon's MCI brought momentum to his church. That's how the story ended, but it began with a knot in Stan's stomach. He was filled with frustration and anxiety as he helplessly watched his beloved church decline. I met him at a restaurant, and he poured out his heart over room-temperature coffee. More than hearing his dismal statistics, I saw despair written all over his face. He felt like a failure and had lost his confidence. He didn't have any idea where to begin. He felt like his best days were behind him.

With every ounce of compassion and tenderness I could muster, I said, "Stan, the first step out of this mess is admitting that what you're doing isn't working."

His expression said, "*You're not helping.*"

I pressed harder. "I'm serious. I'm giving you permission to speak the truth out loud. I've been there and totally understand."

"Troy, you're right. I'm in big trouble and don't know the solution. Will you help me?"

That was when Horizon's recalibration really began.

I've seen it time and time again. The first step for any church or organization that's stuck is for the leader to confront the status quo and say, "This isn't okay." It's crucial to *literally* speak the words out loud:

- "New people aren't even showing up."
- "The morale of our team and the momentum of our church are low."
- "Our staff doesn't even like each other."
- "We spend most of our time on things that don't really matter."

And perhaps the most painful: "If I wasn't the pastor, I wouldn't come to this church."

Yeah, I know. It's brutal, but it's necessary. The goal isn't self-flagellation but to shine a light on the truth. You must be brave enough to see and speak the truth, first to yourself, then to your spouse, and then to those who can be part of the solution. A staff member or board member may be able to start the recalibrating process, but it won't go anywhere until the lead pastor admits the church needs it.

Once you get honest, you can invite your Leadership Community to do the same. It isn't enough to say, "Tell me what you really think. Be honest."

They won't believe you. You must model transparency and honesty. I'm not saying you should hold a venting session, but rather create an environment where your team can openly share and foster holy discontentment.

As you demonstrate your ability to gracefully accept honest feedback and not take it personally, you'll create a safe place for examining every department. Even still, be careful. When we invite people into the process of exposing reality, we can expect them to be self-deceived, self-protective, and resistant to our honesty—just like we probably were at first. Be sure to plan these meetings carefully: spend plenty of time with a mentor or trusted friend who will help clarify your thinking, process your emotions, and chart a path for including others in the discussions.

> **PRO TIP |**
> Inviting your Leadership Community to confront the status quo will test how tightly your personal value is tied to your church's success. Take time to prepare your heart through prayer and seek the wisdom of God. Counseling may also be in order. I have a trusted counselor I see from time to time.

Courageous Questions

Business mogul Malcolm Forbes said, "One who never asks either knows everything or nothing." There are three courageous questions that you and your Leadership Community need to ask in order to cut through all the excuses, rationalizations, and defending of stinky couches. They'll help your team get serious about the work of the kingdom and the future of your church.

I've walked many teams through this process, and I'll warn you: it's brutal. When you meet to discuss these questions, a lot of stuff is going to surface. But don't get overwhelmed—Chapter 5, "Triage Change," will help you sort and prioritize everything. The three questions are the *God* question, the *gut* question, and the *gutsy* question.

1. The God Question

Don't lead your church through any change just because you heard some cool idea at a conference or read it in a book. The bottom-line questions must always be, "What is God birthing in our hearts? What is my divine assignment?" Like Moses, we must say, "If your Presence doesn't go with us, we ain't going!" (Exodus 33:15, more or less). Without God's direction and presence, taking on the giants is a deadly mistake. End of story.

When is the last time you fasted and prayed for divine direction? How long has it been since you bathed yourself in Scripture and sharpened your theology of the church's mission? Do you spend more time reading leadership books than Scripture?

Big warning: Answering the "God Question" doesn't mean telling your people, "I've heard from God and you'd better get in line with my plans!" A better framework can be found in Acts 15. The early church faced a dilemma: some of their leaders insisted that Gentiles be circumcised to become followers of Christ. To resolve the dispute, James didn't act unilaterally but called the elders to Jerusalem to hear from Paul and Barnabas. After he heard both sides, he gave his decree: "It is my judgment, therefore, that we should not make it difficult for the Gentiles who are turning to God" (Acts 15:19— I, for one, am grateful that the church discarded that "cutting-edge ministry").

Then they made this bold decision and declaration, "It seemed good to the Holy Spirit and to us" (Acts 15:28). Before every bold initiative, you need a moment where you can say, "This seems good to the Holy Spirit and us as a Leadership Community." I love the word "seems"—it's both humble and confident. It implies that, while we may not have all the answers, this is what is in the heart of the leadership and God.

All that to say, before you make any significant change in your church, you need a divine sense of God's direction and the support of your Leadership Community. As James said, "It seemed good to the Holy Spirit and to *us*" (emphasis added). Leaders often ask me, "How much do I involve my leadership?" This is a big part of the dance—listening to your Leadership Community without abdicating your responsibility to God's calling (more on this in Chapter 6).

What I'm trying to say is that you need a divine assignment, a word from

God, a nudge of the Spirit. I don't care what you call it, but don't start without it! Okay, that's enough. I'm ready for the altar call. If you need to repent, raise your hand. I see that hand!

2. The Gut Question

The gut question is: "What makes me cringe?" Or let me put it another way. What bothers you? (You can recalibrate your church over and over again with this question.) Acknowledge your holy discontent. Awaken "the cringe factor" in your own life and in your Leadership Community.

I once asked a pastor what made him cringe. He paused for a few seconds, and then he told me, "Troy, I make me cringe. I wouldn't hire me."

"Then that's where you start."

Here are some other pastors' answers to "the gut question" (are any of these painfully familiar?):

- "My website embarrasses me."
- "Young families don't stay more than a couple of Sundays."
- "Our media is embarrassing."
- "My admin can't spll."
- "Our lobby looks like a 1950s bus terminal."
- "I hate staff meetings."
- "I'm not prepared for my sermons and it shows."
- "Did you hear the guy playing the guitar last week? I'm not sure 'playing' is the right word.

So, where do you start? Try this exercise and ask your Leadership Community to do the same. Pretend you just moved into town and are checking out your church.

- Visit the website. Does it make a good impression? Is it easy to navigate? Can you find the service times? Are there directions and a map? Does it say what to do with your kids? (Really, why do churches make it so hard to be a first-time visitor?)

- Examine the social media channels. Are they easy to find? Are they current? What do they communicate about your church? Do they make you cringe?

- Drive to your building, park, and walk around. What makes you cringe about the building, the parking lot, the signage, and the landscape?

- Walk into the lobby. What says, "I'm thrilled you're here!" and what says, "Why did you bother to come?" How does it smell? What's the vibe? Are the greeters the best people for the job?

- Visit the restrooms. Are they outdated? Do they smell? Would a lady be happy with the women's restroom?

- Check out the children's area. Does it feel safe? Would you bring your kids and grandkids there? Are the staff and volunteers cheerful and competent? Are they prepared?

- Enter the auditorium and sit through a service. What makes you cringe about the environment, announcements, worship leaders, ushers, program, and preaching?

- Would you honestly come back another Sunday or keep looking?

Many pastors have a broken "cringe button." It's like having bad breath and not realizing it. It's like having an old couch and not smelling it. These pastors are no longer bothered by the things preventing their churches from moving forward. This is why you often need a coach or trusted friend to tell you, "You have bad breath."

3. The Gutsy Question

The gutsy question is: "Am I ready to lead our church in cultural change? Am I really willing to recalibrate myself, my leadership style, and my approach to ministry?"

In order to honestly answer this question, we must ask, "Why am I here, in this church, with these people, in this community?" Have you fallen in love with your city and your church, or is this just a short-term gig for you? One of the most powerful questions I was ever asked by a coach—you better believe I hire coaches!—was this: "Are you treating your church as a renter or owner?" Renters are temporary and will often treat the house with disrespect. Owners think long-term and invest in the house. If, in your heart of hearts, you aren't committed to spending the next five to seven years at the helm, don't bother starting this process.

I've been at New Life for forty years. As I said, I was saved here. After high school, I became the youth pastor, then the executive pastor, and have now been lead pastor for seventeen years. How have I stayed here so long when the average tenure is three to four years? Because I keep asking myself this painful question: "Troy, are you willing to fire yourself and start over?" What I mean is this. If New Life was my brand new, can't-wait-to-get-started position, what would I change here? What would I get rid of? Then I say to myself, "Jones, find the guts and get down to business!"

With enough Holy Spirit-driven guts, any of us can start over. It's like starting at a new church but without the five years of building trust and credibility. You already know the context of the church and the community. All of this is just a fancy way to ask the gutsy question, "Am I really serious about leading my church in cultural change? So serious that I refuse to let anything prevent it—not even my job?"

You cannot skip this question because it will galvanize *your* soul and give you the core conviction you'll need to lead your church's MCI in spite of the energy and sleepless nights it will cost you.

RECALIBRATE NOW

Chapter 2: Two Offsites

THINK ABOUT IT!

1. Summarize the big idea of this chapter in your own words.

2. What is something new you learned?

3. What is something you disagree with or don't understand?

TALK ABOUT IT!

1. Why are we so reluctant to confront the status quo?

2. If a "secret shopper" came to your church, what would he/she find?

3. Is there anyone else you need to bring into this conversation?

4. Are you personally ready to commit to confronting the status quo? (Don't let anyone skip this question!)

TAKE ACTION!

Personal Offsite: Take a personal full day away from the office to prayerfully answer the "God, Gut, and Gutsy" questions for yourself. Record those answers and set them aside until the one-day offsite meeting (below). You can keep adding to the "Gut" question and thinking about your MCI in the meantime, but don't choose it yet—you need to learn the seven principles first.

Staff Offsite: Schedule a one-day offsite meeting a month or two from now. This meeting will be the "Take Action!" of Chapter 5 (you can peek at it now if you want). You'll invite all the people who will help execute your MCI Launch Plan in Section 2. Why schedule it that far off? Because you'll need to create a working copy of your Strategy Booklet first. We'll get started on that in Chapter 3, but download the template now and get familiar with it: www.recalibrategroup.com/strategybooklet.

3

PRACTICE #2

CLARIFY YOUR CULTURE

"Transform the culture, transform the church."

— *Recalibrate Axiom*

Your church has a cultural DNA. It's who you are and how you "do church." It's the spoken or unspoken mission, values, and assumptions that undergird every decision, every conversation, and every activity. Your culture may have been created by design or was allowed to form by default. If you're leading an established church, then you have inherited a culture that was created over decades.

This alone is worth the price of admission. Don't make any significant changes to your church until you clearly understand:

1. What parts of the culture do you want to preserve?
2. What are the new values and vision you want to create?

Why? Because if you don't first recalibrate the culture of your church, an MCI will do nothing more than slap a trendy veneer over a deeper problem. As Peter Drucker said, "Culture eats strategy for breakfast." The culture of your church can easily withstand and outlast the cleverest of tactics.

The core responsibility of a leader is to clarify the cultural DNA—that is, your church's mission, values, vision, and Mission Critical Ministries (I'll explain these shortly). It's your cultural DNA that provides momentum to your MCI. Without it, your MCI will just be another shallow "idea of the month," nothing more than another church-growth gimmick.

The MCI is like the blade of an ax. While the blade may split the wood, it has little power without the momentum and weight of the ax head, as well as the leverage of the handle.

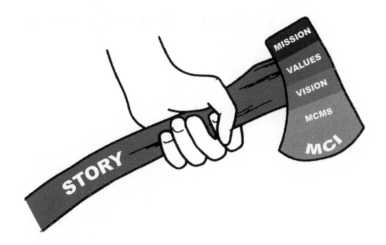

The weight is found in the *mission, values,* and *vision.* These four things represent *who you are* and drive down to the tip of *what you do*—the *Mission Critical Ministries (MCMs)* and *MCI.* Together, they all are wielded by the handle, which is your *story* as an established church. We're going to talk about the elements of the ax head for the rest of the chapter and the handle in the next, but don't miss this point: it's easy to get excited about sharpening the ax's blade, but all its power comes from mastering the fundamentals. You can refine "what you do" until it's razor sharp. But if it doesn't have the weight of "who you are" behind it, then you'll just be scratching the surface, not igniting real and lasting change.

Fair warning: in this chapter's "Recalibrate NOW," you'll add your Cultural DNA (i.e., your mission, values, vision, and MCM to your Strategy Booklet); so read closely, roll up your sleeves, and get ready. There's a lot of important work to be done—but it's well worth the effort.

Now let's take a look at each part of your culture "ax head."

Mission: Your Burning Why

Your mission is the core of the cultural ax head. It's the *burning why* of everything your church does and, without it, your MCI will have no impact. I know, I know. Many of you are saying, "I've heard this before...we all need a mission statement," but hang on for a moment. From my experience, many pastors have not integrated the actual mission of the local church into their own hearts and minds, let alone their actions. Jesus *already* gave us the Great Commission of the church: "Go and make disciples of all nations."

Your mission statement cannot be anything more or less than the Great Commission, reworded to resonate with your culture and church. It's literally the *mission* of your *Mission* Critical Initiative—the entire point of an MCI is to discover what critical actions must be done to accomplish the church's mission. Without mission, your cultural will be insipid and powerless.

Does that mission resonate deeply with you? Is that what drives everything in your church? Does it drive your programs and sermon topics? Your budget? Does anyone in your church actually care about your mission statement or is it just something under the "About Us" tab on your website?

One of the biggest causes of stagnation is losing sight of what you're about. Another word for that is *"mission* drift." The church begins focusing on programs instead of discipleship, meeting the budget instead of impact, cool music instead of experiencing God (yes, you can be hip and still be off mission!).

Start with the Great Commission and craft a terse and memorable mission statement (ideally summarized in a 280-character tweet) that can rally everyone in the church—staff, board, congregation, new-comers, and old-timers. It's your job to galvanize your church around this statement, all the time and everywhere. In membership classes, yes, but also in sermons, board meetings, your announcements, and at staff meetings. Basically, anywhere except weddings and funerals.

This is where the Cultural DNA of your church has to start— with the *mission* and not the *methods*. Don't skimp on this because people can handle changing the *what's* if they know the *why's*. Let me say it one more time. Every MCI must start and end with the mission of the church or it is not "Mission Critical."

> **PRO TIP |**
> Nothing is more prone to mission drift than your sermon lineup. I get away twice a year, in July and December, for a Prayer and Planning retreat to ensure I'm always preaching mission. Don't tell me that "quenches the Spirit"—the Holy Spirit is more present when I prayerfully plan my sermons than when I'm panicking Saturday night!

Values: Your Deep Convictions

Your church's deep convictions provide the momentum of your cultural ax head. No deep values means there is no force behind your culture. Your church's values represent the actual convictions and priorities of your church—which may or may not match the values printed in your membership manual! But done correctly, your values will reflect the unique way that you pursue God's mission. Your values are of the greatest importance to your church. Notice I even put them before vision because values must shape vision.

By way of example, New Life's mission is "Developing fully devoted followers of Christ." These are our values:

1. Authentic Community
2. Biblical Authority
3. Engaging Worship
4. Generous Giving
5. Empowered Church

Just as mission drives values, values drive vision, ministries, and MCIs. Think of the values as the blood of your church—it flows through every part of the body and gives life.

Also like blood, different church bodies have different "blood types." We all have the same root mission but different values. To create your Cultural DNA, you and your Leadership Community have to prayerfully determine what your cultural values *should* be (between four and seven—too many and they lose effectiveness). Your values need to reflect your deep convictions and not be something you've "cut and pasted" from another church.

Again, knowing your values is critical because they give your MCI its weight and momentum. But what if your church's actual values don't yet reflect the values you've set? That's one of the amazing powers of an MCI in concert with the seven practices—they'll help you shift the values to where they need to be. Keep reading!

> **PRO TIP |**
> Don't be afraid to rewrite your values every 3-5 years with each MCI Relaunch Initiative. Not so much the values themselves as their wording. This will keep them fresh and will help you recalibrate your culture.

Vision: Your Clear Picture

Vision provides the ax's direction. My editor, Josh Kelley, told me about when he was a kid and tried to chop some firewood when his babysitter wasn't looking. His lack of control sent the ax deep into his foot. I wouldn't let him show me the scar, but my foot aches just thinking about it. But this is the point I'm trying to make: without vision and a clear picture of where you're going, your cultural ax can easily careen off course.

That said, I'm not a fan of vision statements. A vision isn't a *statement*. It's a clear *picture* of tomorrow that inspires sacrifice today. It should produce the same sort of eager anticipation in your congregation as the Seahawk fans felt when the Hawks were headed to the Superbowl. A well-crafted sentence or two can't do that.

What's the first thing you and your spouse do when you want to remodel your kitchen—write a statement? Or do you look through magazines, watch remodeling shows, and scour Pinterest? Since "A picture is worth a thousand words," showing your church a vision is far more powerful than telling them. Show faces. Tell stories. Show "before and after" images—people learn by contrasts.

One of the Recalibrate axioms is, "See it. Show it. Share it." We'll talk more about this in Chapter 8, but for now, I want to emphasize that you have to "see it" before you can "share it." This isn't just for your church—*you* also need to see it. Visit two or three churches you respect so you can get clarity for your own vision.

Not long after I became lead pastor, I took twenty of my board members and key leaders to Andy Stanley's church in Atlanta. No criticizing, comparing, or sulking allowed. We just observed. Wow! That trip gave us a new, shared vision of what church could be. The "shared" part is crucial. I didn't have to convince them; they saw it. I didn't have to articulate every detail; they'd seen, tasted, smelled, touched, and heard the amazing ministry at Stanley's church. It gave us a picture of the future and saved *years* of me trying to explain this fresh approach to church.

PRO TIP |
Identify two to three pastors who are doing what you believe God wants to do in your church. Learn everything you can from them. Have their numbers on speed dial.

Instead of a statement, I coach pastors to develop a vision *narrative*. It's a one-page document that embodies your mission, strengthens your story, and shares your vision, beginning with the words, "I see a church that..."

Take a moment and finish that sentence for your church. Dig deep. Dream big. Think about your mission and values. Think about your community and the needs you see every time you drive to your office. Think about what you see your church becoming. Say it out loud, "I see a church that..."

Good. Now you have your rough draft.

I continually improve our church's vision narrative by crafting it to make it clearer and more compelling. I try to think in pictures first, then communicate in words. I tell moving, real-life stories. It's my job to move *hearts* so that hands and feet follow. I connect the dots between aspirational goals and flesh-and-blood people. (You can find New Life's official Vision Narrative at www.recalibrategroup.com/strategybooklet.)

That kind of vision—a mouthwateringly clear picture of the future—will provide direction for your Mission Critical Initiative. But without it, Craig

Groeschel warns, "...people become comfortable with the status quo. Later they grow to love the status quo. Eventually, they'll give their best to protect what is, never dreaming about what could or should be."[2]

Do you have a God-given vision for your church? Make sure you have that well set before launching an MCI or else it will just be another ax flying out of control.

> **PRO TIP |**
> During every MCI, have testimonies of changed lives to share along with your vision. Stories help people connect to the why of your MCI.

Mission Critical Ministries: Your Model

Early in my time as the lead pastor at New Life, I learned an important lesson about focusing my cultural renovations. At the time, I desperately wanted to get my church "unstuck" and spent a massive amount of energy trying to fix every ministry at the same time. I got more than pushback—I got conflict and lots of it! Every "improvement" was met with eye rolls, phone calls to board members, and someone else leaving the church.

In exasperation, I told the staff, "That's it. From this day forward, we as a staff are only going to focus on three ministries: Sunday gatherings, kids' ministries on Sundays, and life groups. We'll align all our resources with these three and leave the other ministries on the back burner for now." It was like when Jana and I started to renovate our house, and I told her, "We'll just start with updating the electrical and plumbing and making the house livable. We can deal with the rest as we go."

I didn't realize it, but I'd just described Mission Critical Ministries—the ministries that have the greatest potential to create momentum and fulfill the church's mission, values, and vision. Did it work? Absolutely. While it brought some challenges of its own, this kind of focus allowed me to aim our ax with precision, creating a new culture at our church and bringing growth.

---

[2] Craig Groeschel, *It: How Churches and Leaders Can Get It and Keep It* (Grand Rapids: Zondervan, 2008), p. 42.

But let me repeat: if I hadn't already started addressing "who we are," selecting our MCMs would have merely brought superficial changes.

Clearly identifying the ministries that are critical to our mission has been a key reason that New Life is so effective. It's given us direction for hiring staff and allocating resources, like rooms, volunteers, and money. They are led by our best leaders. When we take out our calendars, the first things we add are the Mission Critical Ministries' events and deadlines. When we recruit, train, and place volunteers, they get the sharpest, most mature, and most available people.

> **PRO TIP |**
> MCM is an effective "behind the scenes" term, but don't use it with the congregation! They'll hear, "Your ministry doesn't matter." Instead, emphasize the Mission Critical Ministries by painting a vision-style picture: "Our church is all about kids. We want this hour on Sunday to be the best time of their week!" You can't say things like that enough.

> **|BONUS TIP**
> Challenge yourself to give a weekly two-sentence "vision-cast" for one of your MCMs every Sunday.

How to Select Your MCMs

You can only identify your church's Mission Critical Ministries *after* you've worked through your mission, value, and vision, but establishing them will narrow your focus, concentrate your efforts, and simplify your strategy. When I coach a church, I never tell them which ministries are mission critical and which are expendable. Instead, we begin by writing all their ministries on a whiteboard, then I draw three buckets:

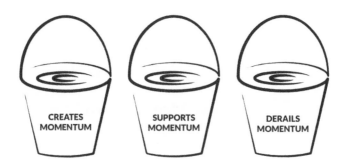

I briefly explain these buckets then have them put every single ministry into one of them. No exceptions.

Create Momentum

What are the ministries that create momentum in your church, fulfill your mission, and align with your values and vision? That's one of the most important questions you can ever ask, and it must be answered before you answer more pragmatic ones.

I once had a pastor ask me, "Troy, can you tell me who I should hire next?"

I answered, "No, I can't. Not until you tell me which ministries create momentum."

He'd been expecting, "junior high pastor," or something like that. I continued, "I wouldn't hire anybody until you've identified your MCMs and then examined your current staffing. You'll know what holes you need to fill."

Over the years, New Life has expanded our Mission Critical Ministries from three to five (which is a good reminder that MCMs are not necessarily static):

1. Sundays
2. Kids Ministry on Sundays
3. Youth Ministry
4. Discipleship (Groups and Classes)
5. Mission and Outreach

That's it. These are the core ministries that provide focus for our cultural ax. I recommend having only three to five MCMs. To paraphrase *The Incredibles*, if everything's mission critical, then nothing is.

Support Momentum

As visionaries, it's easy to undervalue support ministries. I didn't become a pastor to deal with SEO optimization, paper jams, or cash flow reports! But I've learned to deeply value the people God has blessed with the "gift of support," like Aaron and Hur holding up Moses' arms (Exodus 17:8-13). New Life would be dead in the water without skilled people who can handle the operational, organizational, and business sides of the church. Support ministries are, without a doubt, "critical." Mission Critical Ministries can't be effective without them.

However (and this is absolutely critical to understand), the natural tendency of any organization is to accumulate support staff like my teenage daughters accumulated shoes. After enough time, they've added so many support staff, support ministries, and support systems that new vision and innovation become impossible. You need to ask, "Does each staff member create momentum or support it? Do we have ministries that stir up new ideas, or do we merely sustain what we're already doing?"

Derailing Momentum

Perhaps the number one reason established churches struggle is that they squander their time, energy, and money on ministries that don't move the church's mission and vision forward. This is called this "sideways energy." These ministries clutter the calendar and complicate leadership.

I'm sure you can list half a dozen "derailing" ministries without even thinking about it. DON'T PULL THE PLUG ON THEM! At least not yet. The reason these ministries are still around is because they are embedded in deep-seated cultural values. They are what I call "Load-bearing Walls"— cultural values and assumptions (often unspoken) that cause people to resist change. You know what happens when you start knocking down Load-bearing Walls? It isn't good. Architects know how to remove them without bringing the whole house down. (We'll talk about this when we get to Chapter 5, "Triage Changes.")

What About Senior Adults

Any time I talk about Mission Critical Ministries, someone will ask, "But what about senior adults?" Let me be very clear—if you aren't willing to honor your senior adults, you aren't worthy to be called "Pastor." Even if they don't have a designated MCM, it's important to have an effective strategy to minister to them and equip them to serve. I believe that the New Testament commands about "caring for widows" apply to them.

Our senior adults (like kids, youth, and all adults) are seamlessly integrated into our MCMs. We have a beautiful Sunday gathering called Softer Sundays that they love. Our senior adult Life Groups are some of our most vibrant and faithful. Once a month, we prepare a special lunch to honor over 300 senior adults. When I tell the story of New Life, I always include their stories of passion and sacrifice. As a result, many pastors who have visited New Life have remarked that we have one of the strongest senior adult environments they've ever seen. Our church is much richer for it.

This is deeply personal for me. We have a handful of seniors who knew me as a thirteen-year-old boy on the bus. My love for them runs deep. They are my spiritual grandparents. One of the most precious ladies at our church is Lucille Johnson. Lucille is eighty-four years old. She prays for me every day and often calls with a word from God for me. She attends our 9:00 a.m. service, always nodding her head and saying, "Yes" and "Amen" as I walk to the pulpit. Her smile says, *"I'm so proud of you, Pastor."* Lucille is a prayer warrior, a godly lady, and a faithful pillar of New Life.

I reject the idea that you can't reach the young and honor the older brothers and sisters at the same time. As a pastor, I've found that, when the pillars of the church feel loved and honored, they become a strong foundation to help fulfill the mission, values, and vision of the church. They aren't a chain holding you back, but a force moving you forward.

Mission Critical Initiative: Your Igniter

With all the weight, momentum, direction, and focus of the mission, values, vision, and MCMs behind it, your Mission Critical Initiative becomes a tool for bringing lasting change. A finely honed MCI is simultaneously the most and least important part of recalibrating your church. Least, because it is powerless to cut through church's dysfunctions by itself. Most, because without this sharp edge, all you can do is bludgeon your church into splinters without ever breaking through to real change. Church experts will rightly talk about mission, values, and vision, but you can have all those and still not be able to do anything if the edge isn't sharp enough.

That's all I'm going to say about MCIs at this point. We still have four more practices to cover. However, it's imperative to understand that any MCI that isn't grounded in your culture will be all hype, change for the sake of change, doomed to fail. That's the work of an arsonist, not an architect. Transform the culture, transform the church.

RECALIBRATE NOW

Chapter 3: Create Your Strategy Booklet

THINK ABOUT IT!

1. Summarize the big idea of this chapter in your own words.

2. What is something new you learned?

3. What is something you disagree with or don't understand?

TALK ABOUT IT!

1. How would you describe the cultural ax? What's another metaphor for your church's culture?

2. On a scale of 1-5, how closely aligned is your church's mission statement with its day-to-day practices?

3. What's the difference between a vision statement and a vision narrative?

4. Do you agree or disagree that not all ministries are "mission critical"?

5. What are some ministries in your church that create momentum? Support it? Derail it?

TAKE ACTION!

As I said earlier, you're going to create your own Strategy Booklet and MCI Relaunch Plan. In Section 2, we'll work on the MCI Relaunch Plan, but in this exercise we'll complete the bulk of the Strategy Booklet.

Simply put, the Strategy Booklet is one document where you collect the heart and soul of your church. It's an absolutely invaluable tool for staying on mission and describing your church to new staff. New Life has even given it to our website designers so they can better represent us. It should include:

- Your Mission
- Your Values
- Your Vision Narrative
- Your Mission Critical Ministries
- Your Story (this will come from Chapter 4's "Take Action!")
- Your Cultural Voice (we'll get to this in Chapter 8)

You'll need, and want, the full support of your Leadership Community to draft and fine-tune these, so schedule the first meeting right now and plan on two to three more. Warning: This will be time consuming, but don't rush it. Here are some tips as you work on this:

- The best creative work happens when you have two separate "modes," Dream and Edit. Start in Dream mode and write everything, then take a break and switch to Edit mode.
- Identify the best wordsmith in your group.

- Use the "three buckets" to help you determine your Mission Critical Ministries.
- Time brings perspective. Nothing should be finalized the same day it's written. Give yourself three to five weeks to process everything. Sometimes it can take longer, but beware of "analysis paralysis."

Need more help? The Recalibrate Group consultants can help walk you through this process. Talk to one today by visiting the website: www.recalibrateetgroup.com/consultants.

4

PRACTICE #3

TRUST THE STORY

"Yesterday's values are embers for tomorrow's vision."

— *Recalibrate Axiom*

It began as an assignment for my Ph.D.: retell the story of New Life. My business pastor, Randy, and I dug through banker's boxes filled with elders' meeting minutes, monthly newsletters, and annual ministry reports—some of them going back to 1926. We literally read through every single business meeting minutes, many of them handwritten in old-fashioned notebooks. I interviewed all of New Life's former pastors, many of its pillars and influencers, and even flew out to Spokane for one interview. I got a lot more than a fifty-page paper and an "A." I discovered a heart of passion and innovation in my church's story. I learned to "trust the story" for finding New Life's core values and underlying convictions, which I could then embed into the vision for tomorrow.

I was so inspired that we distributed a simplified version of that paper to every family in the church and created a massive timeline mural, ten feet high and twenty-five feet long. Then, when New Life celebrated our 90th anniversary, we created a walkthrough experience, complete with a shabby storefront like the one where the church had met ninety years prior. It was filled with memorabilia and photos. The background music even changed as you walked through the years. This took time and energy but was worth every penny to display God's faithfulness, to honor the saints who'd gone before, and to say to the entire church, "This is who we are! We will always honor the values, convictions, and the stories of the past and take them into the future with us."

Have you ever tried to chop wood using an ax without a handle? Good luck with that. But a nice, long handle, provides leverage and makes gravity work for you. You may not believe it now, but your church's story is the handle that will allow you to wield the full force of your cultural ax and direct your MCI for effective and lasting change.

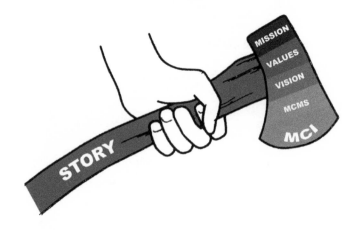

I am convinced that the answer to your problems can be found in your church's first twenty years, when they sacrificed, prayed, and believed God for big things. Your church has a story that needs to be discovered and told. Stories that communicate the values, the vision, and the people who have paid a price. If you're listening, your church's walls can "talk" and perhaps teach you the secret to reigniting your church.

One of the greatest paradoxes of being a cultural architect is that the more things we change, the more we have to clarify what won't change. Peter F. Drucker powerfully communicates this truth:

> Every truly great organization demonstrates the characteristic of *preserve the core, yet stimulate progress*. The job of the leader is to preserve the core, yet stimulate progress at the same time. If you

do one without the other, the organization will become dysfunctional.[3] [emphasis added]

Hence the Recalibrate axiom "Yesterday's values are embers for tomorrow's vision." You already know that living in the past is dysfunctional. We aren't reservationist architects who see churches as nothing more than historical monuments. That's why you bought this book. But refusing to celebrate the past and build upon it—that isn't just dysfunctional. It's arrogance. It basically says, "God wasn't able to do anything worthwhile in my church until I showed up." Never forget that God has been writing a script in your church since before its inception and you are just one chapter of the story.

Your church is where it is today because people believed God and stepped out with bold initiatives. They didn't call them MCIs, but every established church had a moment where the church was galvanized. Moments where someone took a moonshot. Don't see your story as a hurdle to overcome but one to tell and celebrate. Intentionally study the past of your church. It has moving stories that need to be told—the good, the bad, and the ugly. The beauty of your church—and its unspoken values—are hidden in pictures stashed in an attic, stories in the people's hearts, and archives tucked away.

The trick to "preserve the core, stimulate progress" is anchoring every MCI in the story of your church. Grasping the "story handle" allows you to aim your MCI, holding onto the core while stimulating progress. Your MCI Relaunch Initiatives will be richer and more powerful if you can tell the congregation, "We have done this before and we will do it again."

How to "Grab the Handle"

As an example, here are four stories from New Life's story that I've told the church to *preserve the core*. I then explain how I used them to *stimulate progress*. As you read, you will notice how I grab the story handle. Here are the three aspects II focus on:

---

[3] Peter F. Drucker, Frances Hesselbein, and Joan Snyder Kuhl, *Peter Drucker's Five Most Important Questions* (Hoboken, NJ: John Wiley & Sons, 2015), p. 11.

- *The why not the what:* Methods and details should change, but not the motivations. The "burning why" can be the foundation for every future MCI.

- *Principles not preferences:* Your church was founded both on timeless principles and now-dated preferences. Draw out the former without being distracted by the latter.

- *People not programs:* Share the stories of specific people. Use names and show pictures. Tell about the sacrifices they made and the prayers they prayed.

1. Church Plant in 1926

New Life began as a new church plant in 1926 when the Brandt sisters had a vision to reach kids and bring people to Jesus. The church immediately experienced God's favor and, within a few months, they outgrew the Brandt's home. On September 26, they moved to a bicycle shop, but quickly outgrew that and moved into a storefront. It was an old and shabby building—not much bigger than a small house, train tracks next door, and an apartment overhead.

Everyone who attended the small church caught the Brandt sisters' passion for kids, and in 1935, they began a Sunday school program. Because the storefront was so small, the young congregation was forced to think outside of the box and began using a nearby one-room schoolhouse. The leaders would arrive early to light a fire and set up the room. They'd teach Sunday school then dash back to the storefront to attend the eleven o'clock service.

Stimulate Progress:

After telling the church this story, I'll say, "I thank God for a church that loved kids enough to go out and bring them in. A church that was willing to start in an old and shabby building. A church that thought outside of the box because they loved kids and wanted to bring people to Jesus ("why not what"). Kids' ministry is a priority at New Life today because the Brandt sisters injected this passion into our DNA. Our church kept this conviction alive in 1970 when they started a bus ministry ("principles not practice"—I wasn't resurrecting the bus ministry). It was one of those buses that drove to my house and picked me up when I was a boy in 1980. My life was changed because of this church's commitment to innovation and reaching kids who would otherwise not come to church."

I pause and metaphorically grab the handle of the cultural ax and say with deep conviction, "This has been New Life for the last 90 years. Let's continue that legacy. Let's be like the Brandt sisters, who knew how to sacrifice for the mission of God. Who will be the next to think outside of the box? Who's ready for our next moonshot?"

2. Walt Nelson

I'll show a picture of me with Walt Nelson (emphasizing "people not programs") and say, "New Life, I wish all of you could meet Walt. In 1926, he began attending as a thirteen-year-old and remembers the pastor pausing the sermon to wait for the passing train or to go upstairs and ask the tenants to turn down their music. Walt served as one of the first ushers when he was nineteen. For the next sixty years, Walt stood in the lobby and made everyone feel welcomed, loved, and included in the church. He had an uncanny ability to remember each person. They'd return weeks later, and he'd call them by name. Walt liked to say, 'It's easier to win a person with a simple "Hello" than a "Hey sinner."' For sixty years, he served as a faithful usher, loving people one a time as they walked through our doors."

Stimulate Progress

After telling this story, I'll show a picture of Walt and me before he died and say, "Walt made New Life who she is today. He remembered the names of people who walked through these doors. We can only dream about tomorrow because of heroes like him who were willing to love their neighbors with a simple hello. Who will be our next Walt Nelson?" No surprise, sign-ups for greeters always increase.

3. Our First Pastor

In 1937, the Brandt sisters started looking for our first senior pastor. They found William McNutt, only 24 years-old and one of the first graduates of Northwest Bible Institute (now Northwest University). The church continued to grow and see a movement of God and the storefront became too small to hold its vision, so the church purchased a property in 1938. Two years later, a committee was appointed to meet with an architect. The first step was to excavate the basement. Since the church had little money, Pastor McNutt picked up a shovel and began digging the 32 x 48 foot basement himself. "It was slow and hard work," he said, "but I was determined that it would get done, even if I had to do it by hand. After three days—digging nearly eight hours a day—I had a sizable hole."

Stimulate Progress:

When I tell my church this story, I hold up a shovel and say, "The heroes of New Life are people willing to do whatever it takes to move the church forward. Who is willing to get the work done? Who is willing to sacrifice like our first pastor? Who will pick up the shovel and do whatever it takes to reach people for Jesus?"

Then I pause and say, "Our future depends on people willing to say 'Yes!' like William McNutt. We are launching a bold new initiative—who will pick up their shovel with me? Who is willing to believe that the best is yet to come?"

4. The Young Turks

In 1979, the board members recommended that the church look for a new property. The pastor, John Tappero, was sixty-four years old and initially reluctant, but the board had several young leaders who saw the potential of the church. Pastor Tappero fondly called them the "Young Turks" because they pushed the envelope of growth and evangelism. He appreciated having a board that was willing to try new ideas and anticipated growth. In May of 1979, the Young Turks knocked on the door of a local doctor who had a suitable property for sale. Over cups of coffee and a handshake, the board members agreed to buy the property for $855,000. When the doctor asked about earnest money, Darrell Jones (one of our Young Turks) pulled a twenty out of his pocket (which was a real sacrifice for him at the time) and asked, "Will this do?" The doctor accepted, and on that day, the property was sealed by a handshake—in the very same kitchen where Jana and I now make our morning coffee.

Stimulate Progress:

I often stand before church (especially when introducing an MCI) and remind them we're here because of board members who are willing to try new things and confront the status quo. I can point to Darrell Jones, who is still a faithful member of New Life, and say, "I thank God for the Young Turks and the faithfulness of our board. New Life is what she is today because of leaders willing to dream, take action, and trust God for the future." Then, with great passion, I add, "Who will give the next $20 miracle?"

Don't forget to tell these stories in board meetings. I recently said to our board, "Some of you were here in 1979 when we bought our property. It was a huge step of faith. Do you remember? It was our moonshot! Our one domino! Our tipping point. It's time for us to take another step of faith."

> **PRO TIP |**
> Celebrate your board to the congregation as often as you can. This both builds unity and reinforces the value of your board.

There's something else about trusting the story. Whenever I tell a story, everyone leans in and pays attention. It creates an energy I can't describe. We are wired for stories—Jesus knew what he was doing when he told the parables. Put on your storyteller's hat and share your church's stories in your messages, when casting vision, at staff and board meetings, and when training new staff.

I can almost see some of you shaking your heads and saying, "That's great for you and your church, but my church doesn't have any great stories—our 'handle' is totally broken." Perhaps that's true for a few churches, but I just haven't found one yet. Most of the time, the stories just haven't been discovered.

I'll make you an offer: If you read all your church's board minutes and annual reports, interview the five longest-standing members, and still can't find stories of faith and vision, I'll coach you for free. I'm that serious.

Here's one final thought. If you're not moved by the story of your church, don't try to identify your MCI yet. Not only must the church's future be anchored in its story, but you have to love the church and what God has

53

done in it. Without that, the only sort of fire you're going to light is an arsonist's flame.

> **PRO TIP |**
> See yourself as the church's curator. Collect stories and artifacts. Not only can you build on those values, but it will greatly increase your credibility as your established members see that you care about the church's heritage.

RECALIBRATE PROFILE: DARREN SCOTT
Seattle Revival Center in Newcastle, WA

In August of 2019, I met with Pastor Darren Stott and his team. He'd never pastored a church of that size before and needed advice. "I have big dreams," he said, "but not much courage. I'm afraid of making a mistake that will make them crash." Here's what happened:

I invited Pastor Troy to tour our church and give honest feedback. As we walked through the worship center, he said things like, "You need bigger screens. You need a better projector. You need new chairs."

Then Troy asked some great questions about our goals, our building, and our future. I told him we might build a bigger facility in about ten years. He asked, "Why wait? Expand and live in the future *now*." I could tell this relationship was going to stretch me . . . in a really good way. You see, I was always putting things off—two, three, maybe five years. But through his coaching, I realized I was using delays to avoid accountability. Then Troy asked, "What can you do now to have the greatest impact in your church and your community?" "Now" seemed pretty important to him! And I could see how it'd be important for us, too.

He asked about our divine assignment and what made me cringe when I walked through my own church. I had to rephrase that question: "What can we change without causing a split?" As our team prayed and talked, the Lord gave us four big Rally Points for our first Mission Critical Initiative: launch a new service, write a new mission statement, remodel our sanctuary, and remodel our children's rooms. Troy said he wouldn't keep meeting with us until we named our MCI and gave it a date. No more avoiding change! We called it "The Awakening Initiative," and set the launch date for March 29, 2020.

We held a vision night, called "Honor the Past, Engage the Future," to introduce the Mission Critical Initiative. Troy encouraged us to share the story of our church and describe the faith and sacrifices of faithful men and women throughout our seventy-five-year history. Far too often, I realized, we don't root our future dreams in the story of the past. We showed old photos of the church's construction and told stories of risk and courage. It was a wonderful evening. We were all set for a great MCI.

Then the global pandemic happened.

We needed to move the church to online services and only had four days! Thankfully, a lot of the planning and resources for our MCI were exactly what we needed: lighting, screens, cameras, and an updated digital platform. We took one day to plan our next service, another to shoot, and two more to edit. The Lord gave us the idea: a blend of *Mr. Rogers' Neighborhood* and *Saturday Night Live*. In the opening, I came in wearing a jacket, changed to a sweater, put on a different pair of shoes, and then had a conversation with a puppet about how to deal with fear.

We usually had about 300 people watch our services online, but within twenty-four hours, more than 4000 people had viewed our first COVID-19 service. A local television station got wind of what we'd done, and they came out to interview us. We got a lot of traction from that, but none of it would have been possible if we hadn't prepared for the MCI. The cascade of changes was more than we ever imagined.

As I write this, we're still in the middle of the pandemic. When the time is right and it's safe to meet in church again, we'll be ready with our original MCI Relaunch Plan. In fact, I believe we'll have even more momentum because people will be so excited to come back and see each other. The planning and preparation we did for The Awakening Initiative prepared us to pivot and take advantage of the pandemic, and soon, I hope, we can pivot back to the original vision God gave us.

RECALIBRATE NOW

Chapter 4: Create Your Strategy Booklet

THINK ABOUT IT!

1. Summarize the big idea of this chapter in your own words.
2. What is something new you learned?
3. What is something you disagree with or don't understand?

TALK ABOUT IT!

1. Why is the handle of the cultural ax so essential?
2. How well do you know your church's past? Do you think it's been mostly healthy or unhealthy?
3. Are you more inclined to live in the past or look down on it?
4. How does knowing the story help stimulate progress?
5. What is one story you love to tell about your church?

TAKE ACTION!

Devote a week or two to studying the story of your church. Read the annual reports and interview the five longest-standing members, then:

1. Write out your church's "big picture" story in one to two pages.
2. Identify 3-5 key individual stories you can use to anchor your church's values.

3. Add both these to your Strategy Booklet and be prepared to share them at your one-day offsite meeting.

4. Tell one of these individual stories to your church this Sunday and upload it to your website (make sure to get permission from any living individuals you name).

5

TRIAGE CHANGES

"Not everything needs to change overnight."

—*Recalibrate Axiom*

Something that I learned from restoring our house is that remodeling requires continuous triage. That burnt-orange shag carpet may make you cringe every time you walk in the door, but the rat-chewed wires hidden behind the dryer take priority big time. Maybe knocking down that wall would open up the entire ground floor, but you better make sure it isn't load-bearing or else the whole place will fall down on top of you. Likewise, recalibrating your church requires being sensitive to what is important and what can wait. Not everything needs to change overnight.

I was a fairly new lead pastor, two or so years in, when I had a great idea: Let's have our senior high students do more than just attend Sunday school. Let's cancel their class, create home groups for discipleship, and have them focus on our MCMs by serving in the kids' ministry or the main service. We'd be equipping them as young leaders and gaining a new pool of volunteers. It was such an obvious win-win that I didn't bother "leaking the idea" (we'll get to that in Chapter 6).

At the board meeting, I enthusiastically launched into my idea, expecting the board to be as excited as I was. Instead, I was met by blank stares. The more I tried to explain, the harder their expressions got. They simply couldn't imagine discipleship without Sunday school. After all, that was how they'd been discipled.

I quickly realized I'd just swung a sledgehammer at a Load-bearing Wall. I had a choice, either push my idea through or gracefully withdraw it. I knew it was a great idea and could have spent all the goodwill and credibility I'd accumulated to push it through. A big part of me wanted to. But I decided, on the spot, that it wasn't worth the cost and put it on the back burner. Instead, I focused on changing New Life's Cultural DNA in more mission-critical areas.

I learned a valuable lesson that day. Everything has to be recalibrated eventually, but not everything has to be recalibrated now. We have to triage our changes. As one great leadership guru said, you have to know when to hold them, when to fold, when to back away, and when to flat-out run.

Over the next couple of years, I continued earning credibility both by listening to and learning from key influencers as well as by bringing momentum and consistent wins. We started small groups for students and began saying things, like "Students are discipled best in groups" from the podium and highlighted them serving on Sunday in kids ministry (we'll talk about this in Chapter 8).

Three years after that meeting, our senior high Sunday school just happened to come up at another board meeting. One of the board members casually remarked, "With all the students meeting in life groups, they don't really need a Sunday school class. What if we found a way for them to serve instead?" I leaned back in my chair and smiled.

Time to Triage

I've discovered that there are four different kinds of leaders (Strategists, Executors, Visionaries, and Artists—this is the topic of my next book), but right now I want to focus on two of them, each with their own strengths and weaknesses.

Visionaries are naturally inclined to change things. They are pioneers, always moving and unable to wait to implement new ideas. Their weakness, however, is changing things too quickly. They make a grand pronouncement of sweeping changes and rearrange the organizational chart. The board feels bypassed and the staff is confused. This, my friend, is like throwing gas on a bonfire!

Strategists, on the other hand, are inclined to keep things the same. They are settlers, doing a great job of building on what the visionaries started. They manage things well and respect the foundation, but process everything to the nth degree. They spend years talking about changing the bulletin but still haven't decided on a font. They may not ever burn anything down, but they can't light a fire under their church either. Let me add that I've had private conversations with staff, board members, and even spouses who are tired of their pastor talking about change but never doing anything.

As I said, neither of these are bad; we need both types of leaders (and you should have a balance of them on your staff). But it's important to understand which one you are. Where would you put yourself on the Visionary/Strategists spectrum? Would your spouse and staff agree?

Next question: When you're trying to light a fire under your church and bring critical changes to your church, is it better to be a Pioneer, a Settler, or to strike a balance?

Did you answer "balance"? Sorry, but that's the wrong answer. 110% wrong. Balance will kill your church!

Think of it this way: Let's say that there is a major accident on a rural highway. Four ambulances rush to a local hospital that only has one doctor on duty. One of the patients has a huge gash and is bleeding to death. One has six cracked ribs, another a shattered arm, and another a leg broken in several places. There will be nothing balanced about how the doctor treats the patients. The ones with broken bones may be in a lot of pain (I mean, a lot), but they aren't in danger of dying. That is triage. Determine what must be done immediately, then do it.

As a pastor who has confronted the status quo and has a long list of vital changes and who knows which ministries are creating momentum and which are derailing it, how do you know which changes to make immediately and which ones to put on the back burner? By assessing which ones will have the maximum impact with the minimum damage. This allows you to be a Pioneer in areas that are "bleeding out" and a Settler in areas that can wait. When we triage correctly, we honor the foundation while building momentum. We become architects and not arsonists.

Sounds great. But how?

Four Quadrants

For almost a decade, I wrestled with the question of how to triage. Sometimes, I was lucky and intuitively understood which changes needed to wait, like with the senior high Sunday school. Other times…less so. If I shouldn't do everything immediately, then where should I start? I've read a lot of excellent books on leading change, but never found a tool for triage.

Late one night in 2014, I woke up and had a lightbulb moment. It was like 30 years of ministry and research came together in that one moment. I jumped out of bed and started sketching it out. The more I wrote, the more pieces fell into place. It answered every question but was unbelievably simple. Why did it take so long to discover? Why wasn't it in any of the books I'd read?

I call it "The Four Quadrants of Change" and I believe it can revolutionize how you lead—several pastors have said it's the single most useful tool I've given them.

First, some groundwork. Every change you want to make can be charted somewhere on two intersecting continuums. The first continuum is *impact*:

HIGH IMPACT

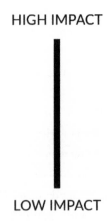

LOW IMPACT

As I said in Chapter 1, the critical question for discovering your MCI is, "What will make the biggest impact now?" Not all changes are equally urgent or have the same impact—that's a foundational principle of this book. *High*

Impact Changes make the greatest difference to your church's mission and the reshaping of its Cultural DNA.

Low Impact Changes yield little to no impact on your mission. This doesn't mean they're unimportant. For example, we determined early on that New Life's bylaws might be important but rewriting them wouldn't make much of an impact (though at your church it might).

The second continuum is *resistance*:

LOW RESISTANCE ████████████████ **HIGH RESISTANCE**
(NON-LOAD BEARING)   (LOAD BEARING)

This is a crucial concept that I don't hear discussed very often. Newsflash—not all changes cause the same amount of resistance! If your church's coffee becomes drinkable, no one's going to complain. If kids suddenly love coming to church, not many will resist. One of the greatest misunderstandings is that people resist *all* change. Yes, most people naturally resist change, but the level of resistance isn't the same. Some changes cause celebration—a pastor "recalibrating" their preaching, for instance!

What Causes Resistance?

Over the years, I've discovered four specific reasons (I call them "Cultural Beams") for resistance. It's important to understand that your members may not know *why* they're angry or resisting change—they just know what they feel. By discovering which of these beams drives their resistance, you'll avoid barking up the wrong tree and be able to respond more effectively. These are listed in order of increasing resistance.

(1) *Budget.* At the lowest level, if there isn't the money for your changes or if people don't see the importance of them, you will face resistance. Furthermore, money represents values, so if you suggest

cutting a beloved program to pay for it, you better believe you'll hit resistance!

(2) *Bandwidth.* Sometimes people resist change simply because they lack the time, energy, and emotional capacity to deal with it. Sometimes, your Leadership Community isn't resisting your great idea, they just don't have the bandwidth to think about, let alone execute, it.

(3) *Beliefs.* Beliefs aren't just theology, they're also assumptions about church and what it's supposed to do. Everyone, even people who don't attend church, has beliefs about church and you'll face resistance if you contradict them.

(4) *Behaviors.* This creates the highest level of resistance. Many people, especially casual attenders, won't give any resistance until you ask them to actually do something. "You want to leave the denomination and rewrite the statement of faith? Whatever. You want me to tithe and host a home group? It's time for us to find a new church!"

(By the way, we're going to come back to these Cultural Beams in Chapter 7—they can be some of your best resources for creating lasting change!)

Load-bearing Walls

In construction, load-bearing walls are exactly what they sound like—they bear the weight of the roof and are essential to the structural integrity of a house. In contrast, a non-load-bearing wall only carries its own weight and can be removed without affecting anything else (but it still might make a mess!). When an architect designs a new building, she can put the walls wherever she thinks best. But a renovation architect must carefully examine the existing structure before moving a single wall. Thanks to remodeling our house, Jana and I know the importance of examining a wall before removing it!

I think you can see how this relates to the "resistance" continuum:

- Non-Load-bearing Walls are things like values, assumptions, activities, people, ministries, and facilities that can be changed or challenged without significant resistance. Moving them may or may not be High Impact, but you can change them without a dozen members demanding a meeting!

- Load-bearing Walls are those things that will face massive resistance when messed with. They may or may not be High Impact, but you will lose a member or two.

Just like an experienced architect can know load-bearing walls by sight, my ability to intuitively discover them has been a "secret of my success." Some of that intuition comes from carefully watching people's reactions when I leak an idea (Chapter 6). If someone's face goes blank or gets red, or if their shoulders tense, it's load-bearing! I didn't realize how much I relied on reading faces until my state's COVID response included mandated facemasks—it was like my superpower had been taken away!

In the next chapter, I'll give you five key questions for discovering if a wall is load-bearing, but as a rule of thumb, it's always safest to start with the assumption that it is. Josh, who is also a former pastor, told me about how he'd been researching communion early in his ministry and came to the theological conviction that wine should be available alongside grape juice (his church already permitted the moderate consumption of alcohol). He ran it by his elders and they approved it without much discussion, so he blithely introduced it the following Sunday and quickly discovered a new Load-bearing Wall! In this case, the resistance was caused by the *felt* beliefs of a former alcoholic. All of his Biblical arguments were useless against the emotions surrounding alcohol. The next week was spent doing damage control and he quickly decided to remove the wine. He said he could have avoided the entire crisis if he had understood that beliefs are more than an acceptance of facts—and if he'd just listened to his wife.

Back to the Four Quadrants of Change. When we combine the *impact* continuum with the *resistance* continuum, we create four distinct quadrants of change:

- Q1: Rapid Wins (High Impact/Low Resistance)
- Q2: Graceful Dance (High Impact/High Resistance)
- Q3: Deferred Progress (Low Impact/Low Resistance)
- Q4: Back Burner (Low Impact/High Resistance)

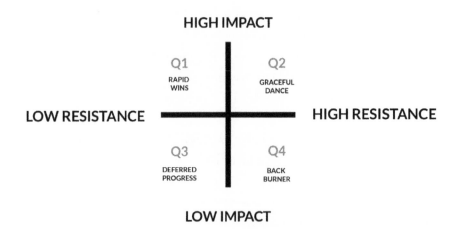

These quadrants will give you and your Leadership Community a new framework and language for discussing change. How quickly will you make which changes? This tool will help you answer that vital question. At New Life, my staff and board will think nothing of calling something a "Q1" or "Q3" change. By thinking and talking this way, we're able to easily triage what needs to happen immediately and what can wait.

I can't tell you how helpful this is. It allows people to rationally navigate highly emotional and complex discussions. It helps your Leadership Community be on the same page—and allows you to recognize when you're not. For instance, if I sense a staff member is frustrated by an idea I shelved, I can ask, "What quadrant do you think this is?" Maybe she thinks it's Q1 (High Impact) but I think it's Q3 (low impact). Then we can have a fruitful discussion, and she might even change my mind!

1. Quadrant 1—Q1: Rapid Wins (High Impact/Low Resistance)

Q1 Description: Cultural changes that strengthen your mission, kick-start momentum, and evoke little or no resistance.

Rule of thumb: Start with Q1: Rapid Wins—find out what it means to win and never stop winning. These may be big or small changes, but keep making them (the faster, the better), especially during your MCI (we'll talk about this in Section 2).

Some people like to call Q1: Rapid Wins "low-hanging fruit." That cheapens their significance—they may have a low resistance but their impact on your church is remarkable. By definition, they're changes that are critical to your mission because they provide the momentum and credibility you'll need to lead other changes in the organization. The first thing I did when I became pastor of New Life was to give our kid's ministry a major facelift. It was a big, significant win. I met little resistance, created excitement, and gained immediate credibility.

Speaking of credibility, think of it like a business banking account. When you're first hired, you're given a "line of credit," i.e. the honeymoon period. However, you have to start earning credibility right away because you'll burn through that line of credit very quickly. If you're a new pastor, you need to understand this very, very clearly—that line of credit is not big enough to cover the costs of all the high resistance changes in your heart. As you seek to recalibrate your new church, be wise enough to back off when you hit resistance.

That said, Q1: Rapid Wins are the quickest way to add credibility to your account. And here's an easy way to "double your money": ask your staff and board members for potential Q1: Rapid Wins. Not only will they come up with some great ideas, but your credibility with your leadership team will also go up as you involve them.

Perhaps even more important than credibility, Q1: Rapid Wins generate momentum and create a culture of change. Think again of a small domino that knocks down a slightly bigger domino, which knocks down another bigger domino (Chapter 1). Each win sets up a bigger win, which is why you should keep rapid wins coming.

PRO TIP |
Be generous with your Q1: Rapid Wins—if you have a new leader, hand them a specific Q1 change. Rapid Wins allow them to build their credibility!

Common Q1: Rapid Wins:

1. Remodeling a ministry room.
2. Painting some walls.
3. Cleaning the bathrooms.
4. Making fewer announcements.
5. Relaunching the Sunday morning children's ministry.
6. Redesigning your bulletin.
7. Replacing out-of-date signs and flyers.
8. Installing new landscaping.
9. Adding signage throughout the building.
10. Following up on first and second-time guests.

2. Quadrant 2—Q2: Graceful Dance (High Impact/High Resistance)

Q2 Description: Cultural changes that strengthen your mission and kick-start momentum, but will encounter high resistance.

Rule of thumb: Only make Q2: Graceful Dance changes when you have credibility and momentum. Even then, proceed with caution. They will make or break your church.

Q2: Graceful Dance changes are where leaders are born (or die). They'll ignite your church, but you risk burning it down if it's done wrong. They are complex and require momentum and credibility—which is why you must start (and never stop) with Q1: Rapid Wins. Don't even start a Q2: Graceful Dance change if you don't have enough credibility in the bank because you're going to spend a lot. If you succeed, you'll get it all back with a generous ROI. But if you're careless and arrogant, you could burn down your church and/or lose your job.

These changes should be seen as a slow and eloquent dance. They're dancing with the saints. You must tread lightly. In the next chapter, I'll show you how to lead gracefully, carefully, and honor your people every step of the way. You will step on toes, but humility will keep you from breaking any bones. "Dance lessons" from someone with experience may even be in order.

Common Q2: Graceful Dance Changes:
1. Making a major change to the worship style.
2. Changing the preaching style or format.
3. Launching or Eliminating a major ministry.
4. Changing the culture of Sundays, especially increased emphasis on reaching the lost.
5. Firing a key staff member.
6. Breaking past attendance thresholds of 100, 200, 500, and 1,000.
7. Shifting the senior pastor's role, especially away from "pastoral care."
8. Changing the governance structure.
9. Messing with denominational traditions and distinctives.
10. Changing the church's name.

Case Study: The Well

There's a reason "major change to worship style" is at the top of the list! We all know how traumatic that can be. But nothing can hold a church back or propel it forward like its music. In many churches, this is the most important Q2: Graceful Dance change that a pastor must make in order to renovate the culture. Knowing how dangerous it is to mess with worship, pastors will often just add a "contemporary service." Done wrong, this strategy will fragment the church's culture and only delay the inevitable. But done right, it can be very effective.

Think of it like this. When an architect needs to move a load-bearing wall, he will often have the contractor build a temporary wall to bear the weight. Temporary walls are a critical tool every pastor of an established church must master. It will allow you to introduce an idea, make tweaks, and acclimatize your church before moving the Load-bearing Wall. Here's how I used this tool to change the worship at New Life without being an arsonist:

New Life's worship experience had been built on choirs and an orchestra for decades. When I first became the pastor, I knew that we had to renovate our worship culture, but didn't have enough credibility in the bank. We decided to add a third service as a temporary wall. I left the two main gatherings alone but added a noon gathering called The Well. At the same time, we started a new gathering called Softer Sundays—a video venue in our chapel with timeless music that honored our seniors.

I told our Leadership Community, "Before I make any changes in the main gatherings, I want to test them at The Well until we're totally comfortable with them." The music had a contemporary edge (and no choir, a first for New Life). We changed the language, the order of service, and "dress code"—I even took off the tie I wore in the 9:00 and 10:30 gatherings!

I really enjoyed The Well. Jeans, no tie, and a sanctuary of willing participants as we tested out new ideas. Not surprisingly, we saw most of our growth there. I gradually (and that's key) added elements from The Well to the other services, all with positive responses. About three years later someone asked, "Why are we still calling our noon service The Well? All three services look and feel the same." Load-bearing Wall successfully moved!

3. Quadrant 3—Q3: Deferred Progress (Low Impact/Low Resistance)

Q3 Description: Cultural changes that don't have much of an impact on your mission but evoke little or no resistance. They can be delayed because they're good enough for now and not worth the budget and bandwidth.

Rule of thumb: Resist the temptation to give too much bandwidth to Q3: Deferred Progress changes. They'll either resolve themselves or move up to Q1: Rapid Wins.

Q3: Deferred Progress changes are little more than a distraction. They take money and bandwidth and give little momentum and credibility in return. Their only "value" is making the pastor *feel* like he's getting something done. It takes an incredible amount of maturity to resist that temptation!

You're able to defer these changes because, simply put, they are "good enough for now." Maybe it will later become higher impact, or maybe you'll have a trustworthy volunteer who really wants to take it on. But for now, there are more mission critical ways to spend the church's resources.

One of these changes at New Life is the carpet in the main auditorium. It has more than a few coffee stains. Every week, my wife and I walk in and she says, "This makes me cringe!" and every week I say, "Don't worry, we'll turn off the lights soon." Jana smiles; she disagrees but smiles. On the other hand, the coffee stains in the lobby were Q1: Rapid Wins because they were so visible and sent a loud message to visitors and attenders alike.

A word of warning: Don't use the Q3: Deferred Progress label as an excuse to be lazy and avoid something that needs to be done!

Common Q3: Deferred Progress Changes:
1. Updating to the latest and newest technology when the current stuff is working "good enough."
2. Cleaning a storage unit.
3. Replacing your database software.
4. Changing a carpet no one sees on Sunday.
5. Canceling a program that has a marginal impact but also costs the church little bandwidth.

4. Quadrant 4—Q4: Back Burner (Low Impact/High Resistance)

Q4 Description: Cultural Changes that don't have much of an impact on your mission, yet encounter high resistance.

Rule of thumb: Have the patience to wait for the right timing on these or else you'll get burned. Focus on things with a higher impact.

Q4: Back Burner changes are a gift to leaders because you won't get a lot of complaining when you say, "Let's wait—we have more important changes to make." Tackling Q4: Back Burner changes will cost you time, money, bandwidth, momentum, and credibility with very little pay off.

The trick is patience. Wait for the right timing because these changes can change quadrants over time. That's because momentum and credibility have a way of shifting resistance in your favor. If I'd tried to change New Life's bylaws the first week I was pastor, the resistance would have been high. But after ten years of credibility-building, it became low resistance. Similarly, I waited twelve years before we changed our midweek boys' and girls' programs. Seventeen years in, and I still have one adult Sunday school class that's on the back burner and that's okay. It can stay there, and I'll keep renovating our culture.

Five common Q4 Back Burner Examples:
1. Changing boys' and girls' midweek programs.
2. Updating or eliminating women's and men's ministries.
3. Rewriting the constitution and bylaws.
4. Refining the membership process.
5. Canceling senior adult classes.

That's it, the four quadrants of change. It's a simple concept. It's intuitive. But if you commit to using it with your Leadership Community, you won't believe how much it will unify your team and focus valuable bandwidth on the things that are mission critical.

RECALIBRATE PROFILE: PAUL GOTTLIEB
Harvest Community Church (Roseville, CA)
Part 1

When I arrived at Harvest Community Church, it was struggling with finances, needed repairs, and didn't have much in the way of outreach, programs, and volunteer involvement—just to list a few problems. In fact, I had to raise my own support in order to go there. And on my first day, the worship leader resigned. The good news was there weren't many Load-bearing Walls. People didn't resist my ideas because they wanted major changes.

The quadrants gave us a language for identifying our priorities. In our team meetings, someone could say, "That's a Q3: Deferred Progress. I'm not sure it's worth the time." This allowed us to quickly gain a lot of Q1: Rapid Wins—paint the bathrooms, get better signs, use name badges, and lots more. We had an adult Sunday school class that wasn't creating momentum but concluded it was Q4: Back Burner. We had enough to do without stirring up trouble!

As I said, people had told me they wanted me to make a lot of changes, so I assumed there were no (or very few) load-bearing walls. After a few months, I realized there were more than I thought. For instance, the church had no central planning, no calendar, and no events scheduling. People used the church any way they wanted. I remember driving to the church one Friday evening and seeing a lot of cars. When I asked about it, someone told me, "We use one of the rooms on Friday nights for Bunko." When I asked people to make requests through the office to use the church, I got a lot of resistance. I'd started a fire that was hard to put out!

As long as I'm at Harvest Community Church, the language of triage will be the way we talk about planning and change. Not only did it help me build credibility through Q1: Rapid Wins, but by clarifying our Q2: Graceful Dance issues, we were able to choose our first MCI.

RECALIBRATE NOW

Chapter 5: Have Your One-day Offsite

THINK ABOUT IT!

1. Summarize the big idea of this chapter in your own words.

2. What is something new you learned?

3. What is something you disagree with or don't understand?

TALK ABOUT IT!

1. Are you naturally a Visionary or Strategist leader? How about the rest of your key leaders?

2. How would you describe the two continuums?

3. How would you describe the four quadrants and the differences between them?

4. What are the four things that cause resistance? Which is the biggest one you've been facing?

TAKE ACTION!

Back in Chapter 2, I had you schedule your one-day offsite meeting. Can it be done onsite, and in several shorter sessions? Not really, or at least it won't be as powerful. Getting off-campus gives perspective and devoting a full day provides focus.

Below is my recommended schedule. Adapt it to your needs, but make sure you incorporate all the core components. (Download at: www.Recalibrategroup.com/onedayoffsite.)

MORNING SESSION

1. Share your heart as the pastor
Idea: Talk about what God spoke to you when you answered the "God, Gut, and Gutsy Questions."

2. Share the story of your church *(from Chapter 4)*

3. Discussion: What do you love about our church?
Write all the answers on a whiteboard and celebrate together!

    Break *(light refreshments, coffee, etc.)*

4. Walk through the Strategy Booklet

    Lunch Break

AFTERNOON SESSION

5. Discussion: What makes you cringe?
Model a thick skin and a joyful disposition—this isn't about blaming people but improving a church. Give everyone a stack of sticky notes. Set a timer for five minutes, tell everyone to silence their inner pragmatists, and write out as many "cringe factors" as they can (one per sticky note). Make this as lighthearted as possible. Offer prizes for the longest, most original, and most "self-targeting" lists. Once that's done, have them select their top five changes.

Now draw the four Quadrants of Change on a large whiteboard and explain the concept to them. Have everyone write, "Q1," "Q2," "Q3," or "Q4" on each sticky note, then work together to prioritize the changes by placing the sticky notes in the appropriate quadrant on the whiteboard. Don't let the conversation get into the weeds. Explain that this is the time to discover, not solve.

6. Final thoughts
In Section 2, we'll dive into the details of an MCI, but you now know enough to start casting a vision for the big things ahead for your church.

7. Pray like crazy!
End your one-day with a prayer meeting, earnestly asking God to recalibrate your church.

6

PRACTICE #5

DANCE, DON'T FIGHT!

"Leading change is a dance, not a war."

—*Recalibrate Axiom*

My first three years as the lead pastor was hell on Earth. Maybe that's a little dramatic, but you can probably sympathize. Yes, the church had grown and good things were happening, but I was losing momentum with some of the church's pillars. Then I got one of those calls every pastor dreads—one of the key influencers wanted to have dinner with me. He said a lot of things that evening, but (to me) it came down to one thing. He was hurt because "his" ministry had been overlooked in favor of our new Mission Critical Ministries.

Even though I tried to go into the meeting with a humble heart, each new attack made me more defensive. I felt the anger growing inside me and my temples started to tingle. Finally, I snapped. There in the middle of River Rock Grill, I stood up and said, loud enough for nearby tables to hear, "You don't know what the hell you're talking about!"

My "righteous" anger carried me out the door in a storm and all the way to my car. As the adrenaline subsided, the first thing I felt was shame, followed by conviction. The Holy Spirit cared far less about my "what the hell" comment than my massive disrespect. Regardless of how he felt about New Life's progress, he was a genuine man of God and faithful saint who deserved respect and honor from me as his pastor.

I called the vice-chairman of the elders—a trustworthy man and another pillar of the church—and confessed my sin to him. He graciously called the other man and set up a meeting between the three of us. I confessed my sin to him and asked for his forgiveness. By God's grace, he forgave me. I asked him to share his concerns again, and this time I listened with a truly humble heart. That's when I began learning to be an architect and not an arsonist.

I don't want to make this sound like a magical ending—it took *years* to rebuild the bridge I burned that day. But by God's grace, our relationship and love for each other were restored and he continued to be an important part of our New Life family. When he passed away, about a year ago, I genuinely mourned the loss but was so grateful for our reconciliation.

Change creates conflict. It's that simple. How you handle that conflict is the single greatest difference between an architect and an arsonist. The arsonist believes he's on a mission from God and heaven help the elder who gets in his way. But the architect has learned to listen before he leads.

One of the most helpful books I read in those early years was Gordon MacDonald's *Who Stole My Church?* Using a fictionalized account, he describes a new pastor with a bunch of great ideas. The congregation welcomed his plans—until they realized he wanted more than superficial alterations and a new program or two. Essentially, he was trying to change the church's Cultural DNA. The book's title comes from an angry member yelling at the new pastor, "Our church has been stolen out from under us!" Reading the book, I saw the faces of my faithful members and realized that I was "stealing" their church. No wonder they reacted! It gave me far more patience and compassion for the people who struggled with my innovations.

Like you, I've been burned by obstinate members, but please put down your torch and hear my heart. To bring cultural change to your church, you must be like the father in the story of the prodigal son. Yes, we're called to reach the younger brothers, but we can never stop pastoring the older brothers. The father understood the older brother's painful emotions—he felt cheated, he was angry. And what did the father do? He affirmed the son's faithfulness, then reminded him of their mission to reach his younger brother. He opened his arms to both of them but used different approaches—that's key.

In short, you must have the heart of a father, not the mind of a ruthless CEO.

> **PRO TIP |**
> Give a copy of Who Stole My Church? to your elders and key leaders. That book resulted in some very helpful discussions at New Life and helped both "sides" understand each other better.

Will You Dance with Me?

My oldest daughter was getting married and it came time to discuss the father-daughter dance. There was one big problem: I'd grown up believing that dancing was sinful. No homecoming dances, no prom, nothing more than a holy shuffle. But there was no way I was missing out on this! So, we decided to take dancing lessons. My poor girl—she should have worn steel toe boots. There were a lot of missteps, a lot of laughter, and a lot of grace, but our special dance that night is a memory I will cherish forever.

Dancing has a leader and a follower. The only thing worse than no one leading is everyone trying to lead—you'll just end up with an ugly mess. But even with one person leading, it's still a partnership. The two dancers must work together and be in sync. Something else I discovered in dancing—the leader's job is to make the girl look good! Even in leading, he is serving. (That's a great analogy for marriage, by the way.)

When you tear down a Load-bearing Wall (a Q2: Graceful Dance change), your approach must be that of a graceful dancer. Imagine this scenario. You have this great idea for a new way to reach people. You lock your office door and type away. You can see it all so clearly: Borrow from this budget. Move this ministry. Then you show up at the board meeting and say, "Starting this Sunday we're going to..."

Instead of looks of excitement, you see surprise followed by questions that quickly turn adversarial. After a very unproductive "discussion," you say, "Never mind. I thought this church was about reaching the lost," and sit down.

Does that scene sound like an invitation to dance or a declaration of war?

A fundamental Recalibrate axiom is, "Leading change is a dance, not a war." I might step on people's toes, but that's never my intention. They might step on mine, and I try to assume it wasn't theirs either. What's the difference? A fundamental assumption: We are on the same dance floor. This isn't me against them. It's us working together to build the kingdom of God.

To be an architect and not an arsonist, you must invite people to dance with you. I recently had a disgruntled board member (we'll call him Rick) request a meeting. It doesn't matter how long I've been a pastor, those words are practically a PTSD trigger. But I've come a long way since that time I swore at River Rock Grill.

When Rick walked into my office, his shoulders were tense and his handshake was too firm. I asked him to sit down. He did so but was stiff and wouldn't even lean back in the chair.

After some small talk, I said, "You've heard me say that leading is a dance, not a battle. I've been told you have some concerns, but I want you to know I honor you and your perspective." I smiled and added, with a touch of playfulness, "Rick, will you dance with me?"

Rick relaxed into his chair with a grin and we began a fruitful (but still challenging) discussion.

The Real Enemy

Let's be clear. There is a war going on, a spiritual one. It is with the enemy of our soul, the father of lies. The very people we're warring with are supposed to be our allies in that war. I once talked to a pastor who wanted to vent about his leadership team. He knew what the church needed to do but they wouldn't get on board.

"They're just a bunch of Pharisees. My entire board," he said.

He looked annoyed when I interrupted him with an upheld hand.

"Brother, these are the people that *God* gave you to shepherd. They've paid a great price for this church and love it. Do you resent Him for them?"

His surprise turned into bright-red-about-to-burst-into-flames anger, but I pressed on.

"They are not your enemies. They're your greatest treasure. Your flock, to love and care for. Don't call them Pharisees because you don't want their input. They're your dance partners and it's your job to gently, carefully, graciously, bring them along."

There aren't many guarantees in ministry, but here's one: viewing your people as enemies will ruin your credibility, cause lasting damage, and make the real enemy very happy. (By the way, if you insist on being adversarial, you better start working on your résumé. You'll need it.)

I'm pleased to add that this pastor humbled himself and I was able to teach him how to dance gracefully. It's interesting, though. Most pastors haven't been trained to handle conflict—so they either avoid it or jump right in with a flamethrower. Sometimes, all they need is a better model and metaphor. Just viewing a harsh word less like a knife wound and more like a toe that's been stepped on mid-dance can make all the difference!

So are you treating conflict as a battle instead of a dance? Here are some telltale signs:

- You start seeing everyone in the church as either allies or enemies.
- You speak in "us vs. them" language.
- You dread staff and/or board meetings.
- You're defensive.
- You find it hard to laugh or relax, even when you're not at the church.
- You find subtle ways to get back at your "enemies," including sarcasm and other passive-aggressive actions.

Four Skills

The greatest (and most common) mistake pastors make when attempting to take down a load-bearing wall is to be a bully with neon orange earplugs. You have to invite people to the dance floor! When people aren't allowed to give input into a new idea, they're 1000% more likely to be critical. Wouldn't you be? But when they feel heard and valued, you'll be surprised how many will dance with you.

As I've said, people will feel violated—like you've stolen their church—when you mess with the beliefs and behaviors of your church. There's no way around that. But over the years, I've developed four key skills that will help you respond with a Father's heart of compassion and honor towards the older brothers. Better yet, they'll allow you to benefit from their perspective.

Take a few days, weeks, or even months to use these skills to explain your ideas for change and the philosophy behind them. Do whatever it takes to get everyone on board. Remember, the goal of an MCI is to galvanize (not divide) your entire Leadership Community; these skills will promote both excitement and ownership.

By the way: it's dumbfounding to me how many pastors resist including their Leadership Community. It can be caused by inexperience, lack of training, pride, or even insecurity. If this describes you, for the sake of your church, do the internal work to deal with it—especially if it's driven by pride or insecurity.

Here are the four skills I use every time I lead New Life in cultural load-bearing change:

Skill #1: Leak the Idea

Begin by asking yourself who you should invite into the dance. Not just those who will agree with you, but also those with a different perspective. Pay close attention to your church's official governance structure and its unofficial key players. Then begin to intentionally "leak" your idea to select leaders, chatting unofficially, and observing responses. Have one-on-one meetings with those who have the most influence. This will allow them to give input at an early stage. That's key, because people will always support what they help create. Identify influencers in your organization and observe their initial thoughts and pushback. Determine the level of resistance. Let me say it again. Don't introduce a load-bearing change without intentionally sharing your idea with influencers and listening to their questions and concerns.

I like to frame these meetings as informal conversations, saying something like "By the way, I've been kicking around an idea...What do you think?" I call this "the conversation before the conversation." It's not on an official agenda, just an off-handed conversation without any rush or decisions to be made.

> **PRO TIP |**
> Influencers and high-capacity people are used to being included at the earliest stages and can be reflexively obstinate if ignored. Don't resent them for this. They've likely earned it. Instead, welcome and benefit from their experience.

Skill #2: Listen (and Learn)

Many leaders get defensive when people show any resistance to their new ideas, but dancing requires listening without having your guard up. Don't be thinking about what you're going to say next. Just listen. Some of what you hear will be brilliant, and some will be...less so. But validate every person who has the courage to speak up.

What are you listening for? First, listen for *insights*. When you ask for others' input—and they believe they can be honest—you'll get a new and valuable perspective about your plan and the congregation's likely response.

Second, listen for *ideas*. I heard about a general who, after receiving a hand-carried report from the field, asked the courier, "Young man, what do you suggest I do?" Talk about humility! But doesn't it seem likely that a corporal had seen something the officers missed? Are you secure enough to ask every person, at every level of the organization, for their best ideas?

This requires the ability to listen to the values hidden behind their words. For instance, when people complain about the volume or song selection, hear that they value worship and want to connect with God. When someone pushes back on an idea, I don't bristle (at least, not most of the time). I calmly say, "Tell me more. What are your concerns?" Quite often, people who appear resistant aren't really against the idea; they just need time to process. They need you to lead them as a gracious dance partner.

Finally, listen for telltale signs of a Load-bearing Wall. Here are five key questions I've discovered:

1. *Who started it?* If the former pastor or some highly influential person in the congregation started a program or ministry, it's probably a Load-bearing Wall. The beliefs and behaviors go deep when a respected person started a ministry

2. *How long has it been around?* The longer it has been at the church, the more likely that there will be deep-seated values behind it.

3. *Will someone lose their job or place of influence?* Pay attention to "place of influence." If the telephone "prayer chain" is led by the biggest giver's wife, that's a load-bearing ministry!

4. *Is this connected to someone's life-changing experience with God?* Emotional attachment creates powerful Load-bearing Walls because people believe that ministry or program must be equally indispensable for others.

5. *How much money has been spent on it?* Money spent can be a huge indicator that something is load bearing. It's a reflection of the church's values.

> **PRO TIP |**
> The "listen and learn" phase is the best time to identify the Load-bearing Walls. Just watch their eyes. That "look" will tell you all you need to know.

But what about when you take a swing at a wall you thought wasn't load bearing only to discover that it was? That, my friend, is when you learn to pivot. I was recently in an elders' meeting and we were discussing how our church would continue ministering during Washington State's strict COVID restrictions. We'd moved our services to online-only and were planning for a much bigger digital impact for the future. At one point, I said, "From this day forward, we're going to be digital-first, in-person second."

"Brother, that won't fly!" responded one elder.

I was taken back by the force of his resistance and felt a defensive my-way-or-the-highway reaction. But then I realized that I had failed to leak the idea. Furthermore, I was so excited that I hadn't come to the meeting ready to listen and learn—I had jumped straight to leading!

I quickly pivoted and invited him to dance with me by asking him to elaborate. As I listened, I realized it was my fault for poorly framing my comments. The problem was language, not values. We had the same values— reaching people with technology. I'd used sloppy wording, so I apologized and asked for a "do-over." I changed the language to: "We want a seamless and integrated relationship with digital and physical gatherings." Immediately all my elders agreed, and we had a meaningful conversation.

In our dance, I'd stepped on some toes with my words, so I backed up and tried again. Instead of getting defensive, I turned an awkward situation into something positive and it was one of my best dance moves ever!

One more thought. As leaders, we don't have the luxury of just throwing stuff out there. When we're sloppy with our words, we confuse people, reduce our credibility, and make people wonder if they can trust us the next time we say something.

Skill #3: Lead

If you've done your job right, all your key influencers have heard the idea by this point and given input. Now, you can lead your Leadership Community forward. You never stop listening, but at some point, being a leader means saying, "There's the hill—let's go take it!"

Here's what I do: create a document that spells the plan out, usually with a couple of options. It must strike a balance between clarity and authority on one hand and flexibility on the other. I present this to my Leadership Community and say, "This is what I think God's calling us to do. However, the best ideas win at New Life, so what are your thoughts? Is this the right direction? How can we make improvements?"

By working from a printed plan, I'm setting the direction for the discussion. They're not being asked to create something from a blank page but refine a thoughtfully-developed idea that they previously helped shape. This is clear, yet collaborative, leadership.

Skill #4: Land

After you've listened to people's insights and ideas, learned their values and perspectives, discovered Load-bearing Walls, and led with humility and clarity—it's time to land with confidence! There comes a time where you have to say, "Here's the decision." If you wait too long, you'll lose momentum, but if you pull the trigger too fast, you'll lose credibility. The

MCI Relaunch Plan, which is the heart of the next section, is effectively my landing strategy.

A Pastor's Heart

If healthy conflict is a struggle for you, then these four skills may be the most important thing you'll learn from this book. As you learn to leak, listen and learn, lead, and land in a way that honors people, you'll be amazed at how they'll buy into your (correction: "your and their") ideas and vision. This process also helps them process their emotions, so they're less likely to feel like someone is stealing their church.

Before we move on, let me be a pastor to you and ask if you need to repent for:

- Acting like a bully and a ruthless CEO.
- Being a people-pleaser and avoiding conflict.
- Only reaching the younger brother.
- Only pampering the older brother.

As a pastor, God has entrusted your *entire* church to your care. Catering to one group, seeking approval, avoiding conflict, or being a bully are different ways that we as pastors are tempted to stroke our egos. As I've said before, the process of recalibrating a church may require you to recalibrate yourself first!

RECALIBRATE NOW

Chapter 6: Get Input on Your Strategy Booklet

THINK ABOUT IT!

1. Summarize the big idea of this chapter in your own words.
2. What is something new you learned?
3. What is something you disagree with or don't understand?

TALK ABOUT IT!

1. When was the last time you were accused of "stealing" someone's church? How did you respond?
2. Briefly summarize the four skills (leak, listen, lead, and land). Which one is the easiest for you? Which is hardest?
3. What are some signs that you're messing with a Load-bearing Wall?

TAKE ACTION!

The first draft of your Strategy Booklet should be done by now. If you haven't already, use it to practice "Leak, Listen, Lead, Land." Move beyond the people who were at the one-day offsite and discuss it with key influencers in your church. Also use this time to create buy-in and get people excited.

There's still one more component to add (the Cultural Voice), but you should be getting close to landing your Strategy Booklet.

7

PRACTICE #6:
RESET THE BEAMS

"Change isn't change until things change."

—*Recalibrate Axiom*

If you ever visit my home and make the mistake of asking how old it is, you're going to end up getting the VIP-package tour. The fireplace was here, but we moved it there. We've extended the kitchen here. There used to be a door there, there, and there. Then I'll pull out the photos because there's simply no way for you to imagine what it was like before. Every square inch of the house has been upgraded at least once. Jana and I have invested a ton of our "budget and bandwidth" to protect the charm of this old home while making it modern and efficient.

The mark of a great restoration architect is for the renovation to be so seamless that everything works together. You may not even be able to tell what is old and what is new. This is the art of restoration. If I could show you "before and after" pictures of New Life over the past twenty years, you'd be shocked because the changes have become normal. We've honored the church's story and stimulated progress at the same time.

As the Recalibrate axiom says, change isn't change until things change. Said another way—change without change is just an announcement. It isn't change when the plan is written or when people have really good intentions. It's only change after it's permanently embedded in the Cultural DNA and people can't imagine what the church used to look like. This is skillful work.

Any idiot can swing a hammer, but it takes an architect to make a change stick and become the new normal.

Without a doubt, one of the most disheartening things a pastor can experience is to pour his or her heart and soul into an MCI, only to discover that the church's culture hasn't moved an inch. Likewise, many pastors have lost credibility because they spent so much time discussing, planning, and attempting change, but they never acquired the skills to integrate the change into their culture. These next two chapters will help you avoid that fate. This is top-notch, rubber-meets-the-road stuff! If you apply these principles, your changes will stick.

What Causes Stickiness?

In Chapter 6, we talked about Load-bearing Walls and how people naturally resist change for four reasons: Budget, bandwidth, beliefs, and behaviors. Here's a shocking principle: The same things that cause people to resist change are also the best tools for creating "sticky change." Think of it this way, when you want to have an open kitchen, you must remove one beam and bring in another; the old beam was stopping change and the new one will strengthen it.

Just as every building has beams that hold a tremendous amount of weight, every church is held together by the Cultural Beams of budget, bandwidth, beliefs, and behaviors. As you recalibrate your church, they'll be a double-edged sword. Try to move a Load-bearing Wall without also resetting the beams and the church may come crashing down. But if you can carefully and intentionally move the beams, your church's entire culture will move as well.

Do you see what I'm saying? The very same resistance that you'll face when you try to recalibrate your church can be what keeps it from drifting back to the old way of doing things. The same glue that can hold things in the wrong place can also hold them in the right place. In fact, if I come up with some "bright new idea" that doesn't fit with New Life's new culture, I'll encounter resistance from my own team—and that's a good thing! This has been a major secret to our success.

Resetting your budget, bandwidth, beliefs, and behaviors around your mission, values, vision, and Mission Critical Ministries is tough work. It will require time, wisdom, and many painful decisions. But no lasting change can happen without it.

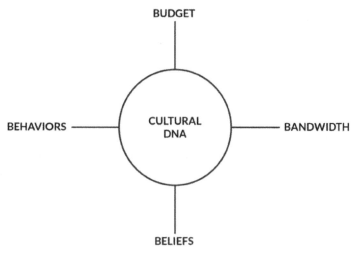

1. Budget: Put Your Money Where Your Mouth Is

Show me your budget and I'll tell you what your culture actually is. You can't say "We value kids!" and not spend money on great staff, a fun environment, and a quality program. When I became pastor of New Life, I knew that our Children's ministry was one of the most important parts of the church, but we spent more on our annual Christmas production than on them! Our budget said, "We value musical production more than children's ministry." That might be okay if you're pastoring a church of snowbirds in Tempe, but not for New Life. So we trimmed our musical production and redirected that money to our kids. Did that ruffle some feathers? Absolutely, but the first step to making change stick is resetting the cultural beam of budget by putting your money where your mouth is.

Maybe you're thinking, "That's easy for you to say—you're a big church with lots of money!" A bigger church may mean more money, but it also means even more expenses. All churches, New Life included, have limited budgets and have to make hard choices to align their spending with their mission, values, vision and MCMs. When we draft our annual budget at New

Life, it is driven by our Mission Critical Ministries. Knowing our MCMs makes the painful decisions simpler (but not any easier!).

As with any Load-bearing Wall, don't try to revamp your entire budget overnight. Start with gathering the facts. Print up your budget and be brutally honest—what does it say about your values? Begin teaching your Leadership Community to talk in terms of culture, the quadrants, and MCMs whenever you discuss money. Start doing that now, well before it's time for the annual budget. And with each new budget, look for ways to carve out more money for your MCMs.

> **PRO TIP |**
> Make sure your budget is organized by ministries. Even if your payroll is lumped together, ask for reports that allow you to evaluate what the salaries say about your values. Bonus points if you notate "Creates/Supports/Derails Momentum" — just don't publish it in the congregational report!

2. Bandwidth: Focus Time and Energy on the Things That Will Make the Biggest Impact

Bandwidth—the sum of your available time, energy, drive, and heart—is your church's most precious resource. More MCIs crash and MCMs fail to thrive because of insufficient bandwidth than budget. To bring lasting change, you must intentionally focus your church's bandwidth on the things aligned with your Cultural DNA. Just as your personal, unplanned time tends to flow into your smartphone and television, bandwidth will not naturally flow towards your priorities. You must budget it like money.

Examine your MCMs carefully. You can't say you value discipleship groups if they don't get a generous portion of the church's bandwidth. Here's another Recalibrate axiom: Say "no" to good things so you can say "yes" to mission-critical things.

Your church has four types of bandwidth that must be actively managed:

a) Communication bandwidth

Announcements, church mailings, and prime website placement do far more than inform. They communicate what's important. I can tell what a church values based on the Sunday morning announcements. Which ministries get "airtime"? Similarly, if a church has a 15-minute blast of announcements from a wide range of ministries, it tells me that the pastor hasn't identified his Mission Critical Ministries (or that he's afraid of conflict).

Bandwidth also applies to the congregation's attention span. They can only hear so many announcements before they stop listening. That's why New Life chooses its announcements very carefully and views them as an opportunity to either shift or reinforce a Cultural Beam. Will a single announcement permanently change the church? It's doubtful, but when every single announcement is nudging the bandwidth beam, it will slowly move.

b) Volunteer bandwidth

We forget our volunteers have lives outside church! While we should always try to bring in new volunteers, recruiting for one ministry frequently means stealing from another. Make sure that your MCMs get the lion's share of the volunteers. Obviously, this doesn't mean pushing volunteers into a ministry they hate. It means casting vision for your MCMs' needs and nudging new volunteers towards those.

c) Facility bandwidth

The moment I walk onto your campus, I know what you value—regardless of what the mission statement says. Which ministries' facilities get the professional touch and which ones get the donated couches? Furthermore, facilities also have a bandwidth of their own. If two different ministries want to use the same room, who wins? Your buildings and your scheduling policies reflect your values. Resetting this beam will be tough because it will make a lot of people unhappy, but you need to reframe your facilities around your Cultural DNA.

d) Staff bandwidth

Staff members also have limited bandwidth. This is why I always ask, "Are we putting our staff's energy into the MCMs? Or has it been derailed by things that don't have the greatest impact?" And, of course, I ask the same thing of myself. Most of us have a to-do list, but we just as desperately need a stop-doing list. When we eliminate good things so we can focus on the essential things, we make more progress on the things that matter.

3. Beliefs: Lead with the "Why" Not the "What"

As I said, beliefs don't only mean your church's "Statement of Faith." Beliefs are the sum of your congregation's underlying assumptions, values, and ecclesiology (even if they don't know what "ecclesiology means). Said another way, beliefs are your church's answer to the question, "What is the church supposed to do?" And the answer to that is so big and so deeply ingrained that no mission statement can address it.

As I'm writing this, our country is heading into perhaps the most dramatic election I've ever witnessed. Last week, twenty minutes before service started, one of my long-time members marched up to me, "Why don't you stand up there and tell these people that [my candidate] has to win?" he demanded. "Why won't you stand up for truth?"

He was so aggressive that Jana stood next to me to provide emotional support. I was tempted to argue with him, but instead of confronting the "what," I addressed the "why." Our church is about the gospel, about making fully devoted followers of Jesus and reaching all people regardless of their politics. I told him that everyone—republican, democrat, or other—has a place in the church and that I'm more concerned with Kingdom principles than political ones. (I know some of you are cringing right now—I'm hitting a Load-bearing Wall, aren't I?) He kept trying to sidetrack me, but I kept the main thing, the main thing. The reality is that he had a different belief about what the church is supposed to be doing, and I wasn't about to change our church's belief ("we're about the gospel, not politics") to make him happy.

While all the other Cultural Beams tend to be practical, this one gets very personal. When you mess with it, you are messing with people's very core. To make it even trickier, most people haven't examined their assumptions.

They just know how church is *supposed* to be done. The role of church in politics is one such belief. Some others are:

- How are pastors supposed to act and what are they supposed to do?
- What is the church's responsibility to the poor, the lost, and the saints?
- Is the church a democracy?
- How are we supposed to worship?

So, how are you supposed to reset the belief beam? It is a long-term, ongoing, two-prong approach:

First, lead with the *why* not the *what*. Whenever your renovations are met with resistance and hostility, don't get drug into a fight over practices. Take the time to uncover the assumptions and values that are driving the conflict. Focus on those. Draw the conversation back to values and principles, not programs and preferences.

Second, change the language of your church. This may surprise you, but the key to beliefs is language. We'll talk a lot more about this in the next chapter, but almost every time you open your mouth is an opportunity to reset the belief beam.

PRO TIP |
Staff, board, and volunteer meetings provide a great opportunity for changing the culture of your leadership. Take a couple of minutes in every meeting to reinforce a key belief. Even better, always be reading a book together and invite others to lead the discussion.

4. Behaviors: Celebrate Today What You Want to Become Tomorrow

The most difficult cultural beam to change is behaviors, but it isn't optional—change isn't change until it's reflected in how the leadership and the congregation act. Behavior creates and reflects the Cultural DNA of your church. It's one thing to declare, "We're a warm and inviting church!" but the real question is "Do visitors feel welcomed?" Ask the tough questions:

- If you say you value prayer, are people actually praying?
- If you say you value missions and outreach, do people invite their friends to church?
- If you say you value kids' ministry, do you encourage your best and brightest volunteers to serve there?
- In short, do your actions line up with your mission, values, vision and MCM's.?

So, how do you reset the behaviors of your staff and church? The first and most obvious (and most painful) answer is that you as the leader must change your own behaviors. As leaders, we teach what we know and reproduce who we are. I know we all have hundreds of excuses, but you must be doing what you want your people to do. It is that simple.

Second, you need to hold your Leadership Community accountable. Inspect what you expect. I know this isn't fun, but that's leadership. And when it comes to your paid staff, you are also their boss. Making them do *their* job is literally *your* job.

Finally, when it comes to the congregation, you have a lot less authority (you can't fire them), but you still have influence. Your preaching shapes the culture of your church more than anything else. But if sermons were enough to change behavior, every church would be filled with perfect people. One of the best tools I've discovered for changing behavior is "Celebrate today what you want your church to become tomorrow." I'll talk more about this in the next chapter, but if you consistently praise the specific behavior that lines up with the mission, values, vision, and MCM's of your church, you will watch it become more common.

High Impact Decision Making

As I was writing this book, I asked my editor about including a diagram with a blue line, to mimic the blue line on my phone's GPS. He texted, "We could do that, but: 1) Adding color would increase costs, 2) we'd need to rework the rest of the diagrams, so they match, and 3) you'd want to make sure it's helpful enough to be worth all of the above!"

I texted back, "Okay, let's skip it." But notice how the four Cultural Beams came into play:

- Budget—is the diagram worth the extra cost?
- Bandwidth—is it worth the time and energy?
- Beliefs—do we believe it will impact the readers?
- Behavior—should we do it?

We got a chuckle out of that, but it highlighted how intuitively I've learned to filter my decisions through the Cultural Beams. This is "high impact decision making," a crucial skill for recalibrating your church. Here are seven examples of how New Life has made high impact changes, specifically in regards to our Mission Critical Ministries, to reset and reinforce our Cultural Beams.

Decision #1: Hire staff around our Mission Critical Ministries

Whenever we launch a new campus, the campus pastor is our first hire. But second is usually the children's pastor, even if it's initially part-time. That's right—we don't hand the kids off to a college intern. They get their own dedicated pastor.

    Cultural Beam: **Budget**

Decision #2: Invest in the environments of our Sunday MCMs

By environment, I mean the total "feel" of the space. The lobby communicates warmth and authenticity. The coffee is good. The greeters have been well trained. And our commitment to children is obvious from the "Kids' Town" sign that's bigger and nicer than the church's.

    Cultural Beam: **Budget, Bandwidth**

Decision #3: MCMs' announcements get priority

If the children's ministry and a book club both want the last open slot for an announcement, the decision is already made. And when we make the announcement, we make a point of reinforcing our beliefs. For instance, when it comes time to announce the dates for camp, we will say, "Kids are the heart of our church. They're the next generation of disciples and leaders, and we're committed to families growing in their faith. We're getting ready for our next vacation Bible camp, and you can be a part of changing a child's life by serving or giving a scholarship." Then I tell the story of New Life paying $55.00 for me to go to Bible Camp—you better believe that makes for effective fundraising!

Cultural Beams: **Bandwidth, Beliefs, Behaviors**

Decision #4: Focus our staff on MCMs and MCIs

If a staff member ever says that they don't have time for a Mission Critical Ministry or Initiative, they'll be asked, "Is there anything less mission critical you can take off your list?" It isn't enough to hire for our MCMs, we all have to continually refocus our energy.

Cultural Beams: **Bandwidth, Behaviors**

Decision #5: Rally our volunteers towards our MCMs

When other pastors visit New Life, they often remark on how many incredible parking lot attendants, greeters, ushers, and kids' ministry workers we have. The truth is that we don't have a ton of volunteers. I think we need to step up our "volunteer culture" game. What we have are *focused* volunteers. They're all rallied around our MCMs, which is why it appears we have so many.

Cultural Beams: **Bandwidth, Behaviors**

Decision #6: Build our facilities around MCMs

When we built our new facility, we got a flood of requests from people who wanted various amenities included in the design. However, our MCMs gave us criteria for making those decisions and we chose *not* to build:

- A room for the choir and orchestra
- More offices for pastors
- Adult Sunday school rooms
- A bookstore/resource center

- Athletic club/workout facility
- A wedding chapel

Instead, we gave our MCMs whatever they needed and we poured money into their building design—the entire look of our children's area shouts, "We love kids!"

Cultural Beam: **Budget**

Decision #7: Use our "preaching time" to reinforce MCMs

Our MCMs get more than lip service in our membership class; we integrate them into sermons and announcements. Not just through teaching, but also by celebrating our successes. So in a sermon, I might say something like "What I love about New Life is our heart for missions. This church's heart breaks for the things that break the heart of God," then I'll tell a story that connects the dots to our mission today.

Cultural Beams: **Beliefs, Behaviors**

Case Study: New Life's Choir and Orchestra

I don't want to leave you with the impression that moving Cultural Beams can be painless. If it was easy, it would've already happened. Ministries that you deem non-MCM are led by people that love God and are devoted to their work—often fiercely. I'm not telling you anything new. In my "Recalibrate" seminars, I can see pastors clench their teeth when I talk about momentum-derailing ministries (Chapter 3) and selecting their MCMs. In their gut, they can feel the price they'll have to pay. I feel it with them because I've paid it too.

I'd been at New Life for a few years when we decided it was time to tackle the Load-bearing Wall of renovating our worship culture. I already talked about this in Chapter 5's case study ("The Well"), but I left something out, something that still hurts a little. For years, New Life had its very own orchestra and a choir, filled with very talented people dedicated to leading beautiful worship. But, as The Well took the church in a more contemporary direction, it felt more and more out of place.

It finally came down to an issue of budget and bandwidth, but I was also up against the belief that a church must have a choir, not to mention forty years' worth of behavior. In fact, I still have fond memories of the singing Christmas trees from way back when. But Mission Critical Ministries were suffering because of the choir and orchestra. Something had to change. It's a long and painful story that includes many unsuccessful—and unwelcome—attempts to update the choir. Much of what I now know about Load-bearing Walls (Chapter 7), honoring the past (Chapter 4), and dealing with conflict (Chapter 6) was forged from my failures here.

I finally made the tough call. The choir and orchestra had to be cut. Jana recognized how painful it was for me and offered to break the news. My wife is an amazing singer and worship leader (I married up) so she had already developed a connection with them. She gathered everyone together, explained the church's new direction, then gave them the news. As much as they appreciated Jana's heartfelt communication, they were still very hurt. It was a brutal season for me. Many left the church. One person asked, "How can you do this? How can you steal my ministry after all these years of faithfulness?" All I could do was swallow hard, communicate the values again, and hope the flames would subside.

So, when I see pastors that I'm coaching react to the thought of cutting ministries, I understand. I assure them they don't have to bring out the ax the day they get home. And I never tell them which ministries are expendable. I simply focus on the MCMs and support ministries, then leave it up to them to figure out what's derailing momentum.

RECALIBRATE PROFILE: STAN RUSSELL
Horizon Community Church, (Tualatin, OR)
Part 2

I introduced Stan Russell in Chapters 1 and 2. Let's continue his story:

When Stan launched his first MCI, "Horizon 2.0," the plan required repositioning a couple of people and hiring another staff member. Their dreams were huge, and they realized they didn't have the bandwidth or budget to do it all at once. They began phasing in the changes over eighteen months, giving them time to start moving their Cultural Beams.

One of the decisions, driven by the "facility bandwidth," was to transition from adult Sunday school to midweek Life Groups. "We needed more rooms for our growing kids' ministry," Stan explained. "This challenged a deeply rooted belief that discipleship happens best on Sunday mornings in large groups. We had to actively teach that small groups were better because it allowed people to be more vulnerable and apply the Scriptures to particular life issues."

Changing the beliefs and behaviors beams is challenging work and one key leader wasn't happy about it. Stan met with him for three years to help him warm up to the new strategy. In the end, the man and his wife left the church and took other couples with them. Stan was sad to see them go, but said, "If we'd tried to keep the Sunday school classes and add small groups, they both would've been mediocre."

Horizon 2.0 has been followed with a new MCI every year. Each one begins with Stan and his team taking the time to ask the God, gut, and gutsy questions (Chapter 2). He says, "These questions lead to wonderful discussions, which bring us back to the Lord, make us more objective, and give us the courage to take steps of faith."

RECALIBRATE NOW

Chapter 7: Reset Your Budget and Bandwidth Beams

THINK ABOUT IT!

1. Summarize the big idea of this chapter in your own words.

2. What is something new you learned?

3. What is something you disagree with or don't understand?

TALK ABOUT IT!

1. How can something both create resistance and stickiness?

2. How would you describe bandwidth?

3. What are some things that you can stop doing now to give more bandwidth to your MCMs?

4. What are some beliefs that are limiting your church right now?

TAKE ACTION!

You've probably preached about how "checkbooks and calendars" reveal true priorities. Now apply that principle to your church. Print out your church's budget (including itemized salaries) and calendar (with events and facility usages, if possible). Pretend to be an outsider and ask what they actually say about your church's priorities.

If you don't like what you find, create a plan for incremental change.

8

MAKE IT STICK!

"Language creates culture."

— Recalibrate Axiom

Transform the culture, transform the church. It's that simple. But how do you do it?

I'd been New Life's lead pastor for less than six months and was busy making all sorts of changes. Or at least I was trying to. I'd made progress on my Q1: Rapid Wins, but was struggling to move the Cultural Beams, especially the belief beam. Only I didn't know any of that—I just knew I wasn't seeing DNA-level change.

One evening, I was walking around the streets of downtown Kirkland with a couple of friends and discussing church growth. One of them—a real philosophical, geek-type guy—didn't say much, but I could see his wheels turning. Suddenly, he stopped walking in the middle of the street and said, "Language creates culture," then he kept walking. That was it. Three words that changed everything. I like to say that I was "born again" as a leader at that moment.

I realized I was trying to change the beliefs and behaviors of the church but wasn't anchoring those changes in the church's language. The next Sunday, I stood up in front of the church and said, "You know what I love about New Life? We're a church that reaches the unchurched. That we love and reach out to young families." From that point on, I started telling stories about our values as often as I could.

I was shocked to see how effectively this language changed the beliefs and behaviors of New Life. It created a culture of reaching out to the unchurched. The more stories I told, the more the church lived up to those stories. People started to invite friends. The staff started thinking more about the unchurched as they planned our services. I wrote my sermons with the knowledge that unchurched people would be listening. People started to get saved and baptized.

As I said in Chapter 3, a key Recalibrate axiom is "Transform the culture—transform the church." The Cultural DNA of your church is created by language, so whoever shapes the cultural voice, transforms the church. In *Cracking Your Church's Culture Code*, consultant Sam Chand explains, "Words have the power to shape lives and organizations. Too often, however, leaders aren't aware of their vocabulary as they speak, and they don't realize how people are affected by their words. Even casually spoken statements can have profound effects. The words we use, and the way we use them, define organizational culture."[4]

When I say *language*, I'm referring not only to the actual words. I'm talking about tone, timing, body language, metaphors, and imagery. Successful companies get this. Disney calls their customers "guests" and they don't have "employees," they're all "cast members." People flock to Chick-fil-A, in part, because their staff is trained to smile and say, "It's my pleasure to serve you." And they mean it. A company can even change an entire nation's language. Before Starbucks, coffee came in small, medium, or large. Now it's "tall," "grande," and "venti." These things aren't mere semantics. Language determines the Cultural DNA, shapes relationships, and predicts outcomes.

To reset Cultural Beams (especially beliefs and behaviors) and make your renovations stick, you have to create a new cultural language for your church. I say "new" because every church already has a default cultural voice and language. The only question is if *that* language reflects your mission, values, and vision (Chapter 3). Does it help you reach outsiders, or does it alienate them? Does it honor the pillars of your church, or dishonor them? Does it

---

[4] Samuel R. Chand, *Cracking Your Church's Culture Code* (San Francisco: Jossey-Bass, 2010), Chapter 4.

empower people, or make them dependent on you? Does it provide hope, or create tension? Does it bring glory to God, or yourself?

> **PRO TIP |**
> Try to eavesdrop on at least two conversations every Sunday. Don't talk, just listen to discover your church's actual cultural language. Do the same thing before staff and board members—pretend to read your notes as you listen in.

Four Tools of the Cultural Architect

Culture is shaped through language. So, what kind of culture are you creating? That's the question every pastor and Leadership Community must wrestle with. When I coach pastors, I tell them, "Send me a link to one of your services. I'll listen to the music, the announcements, the greeting, the message, and the prayer. In one service, I'll hear the cultural voice of your church. Your language will show me more about your church's Cultural DNA than anything else."

> **PRO TIP |**
> Find an insightful person to listen to one of your services and tell you what values they heard.

The irony is that preachers get paid to talk, but many of us haven't harnessed the power of language to make change stick. There are the four tools I use as a cultural architect to anchor MCIs in our mission, values, vision, and MCMs.

1. Connect the Dots

About eighteen months into my time as the pastor at New Life, I could feel a storm brewing in the church. I'd stopped preaching expository three-point sermons and transitioned to a more conversational and engaging style. Even though my sermons were just as biblically-based as ever, people started asking, "Is New Life compromising? Are we selling out in the name of church growth?" I started receiving emails complaining "You don't preach the Bible" and the cringe-inducing "I'm not getting fed."

I'm not proud of it, but I responded to one such email with a list of all the Scriptures I had preached in the last eight weeks. I wasn't trying to dance with the sender (Chapter 6); I was just proving that I was right. But my childish response made me realize that I'd forgotten "language creates culture." One Sunday shortly afterward, I stood in front of the church and said, "From time to time, people ask what we preach around here. I tell them, 'We preach the Bible. Cover to cover. Sunday after Sunday.'" This was a quote from one of New Life's values and the room came alive as I connected the dots between my sermons and our cultural value of Biblical Authority. Once the dots were connected, the complaints started to fade. By the way, I still say this in my messages.

Here's a key point. You deal with this stuff day in and out; your congregation only thinks about it for an hour on Sunday. Just because the connection is obvious to you doesn't mean it's obvious to them. It's your job to continually connect the dots between your church's activities and the Cultural DNA you're trying to reinforce. Otherwise, they just see a bunch of activity unrooted in purpose. This isn't an instant fix but done consistently over the long haul, it will change the beliefs and behaviors of the church.

Talk about your values constantly and connect them to everything you do, or else they won't ever become a true Cultural Beam. Even if it feels awkward at first, begin your staff meetings and board meetings with a reminder of one or two of your values. Weave them into your sermons and announcements. But perhaps your most powerful way of connecting the dots is telling stories. Here's one I told to my congregation:

> I see a church that warmly welcomes people who have no interest in church or the gospel. I see a church where unchurched people love to come. I see a mom and her two little children getting up early and coming to New Life, as they do every Sunday. But for some unknown reason, her husband decides to join her. She's been praying for this, but never really thought it would happen—he always has some excuse about work or football. She's a little afraid and a little hopeful.

By the time they pull into the parking lot, he's already questioning his decision and is looking for a reason to leave. She sees some smiling people nearby and hopes one of them is a normal guy who can connect with her husband. When she walks through the door, her anxiety increases with every step and she prays no one will say anything stupid to him. Maybe a football fan will talk Seahawks with him instead of kicking him out for wearing a Russell Wilson jersey to church!

As she drops off her baby, she hopes the nursery is staffed with friendly adults who will make a good impression on her husband. When she gets to Kid Town, she prays that her husband will notice her five-year-old son's excitement. They walk into the auditorium and sit near the back. She's still nervous and he's on edge. All she wants is for her husband to like it, and just maybe, that he'll want to come back. What if they could be one of those families that goes to church together? But that's so much to wish for...

She starts praying that the music is good and that the sermon isn't about tithing. When I start preaching, she hopes her husband will respect and perhaps even like me. She also hopes that I won't say anything that would give him a reason to never return. She prays for a moment of laughter, that I'll be honest and authentic about what it means to be a follower of Jesus, and that somehow her husband's heart will be touched...

At that point, I paused and looked straight at our people and connected the dots:

This actually happened—she shared her story with me last week. This is what church is all about. We are the way God answers the prayers of this wife and mom. Everyone from the parking lot attendants to those in the children's ministry, to the greeters and ushers, to the worship leaders and the preaching—we're all working together with this praying mom to reach her husband for Jesus.

By the way, this is why it's so important to create your Strategy Booklet (you have been doing the "Recalibrate NOW" exercises, right?) and always have it on hand. If you're ever in doubt about how to open up a meeting or a message, refer to your Strategy Booklet for your values!

> **PRO TIP |**
> If you have a template you use for Sunday services, add to it "Which value will I reinforce today?" Be intentional about cycling through each of your values.

2. Celebrate Wins

One of the greatest tools of the cultural architect is celebrating wins. As I said in the last chapter, *celebrate* today what you want your church to become tomorrow. Loudly and intentionally celebrate the beliefs or behaviors you want to reinforce. For example, at New Life we celebrate:

- When people are baptized.
- When people have devotions.
- When people invite friends.
- When people serve in kids' ministry and the parking lot.
- When people are Jesus to their community and the world.

But when you scold your church for not volunteering in the nursery and focus on the negative, you create a toxic culture and dishonor God. I recently asked a pastor I was coaching about his most recent Sunday. "No one new came," he said despondently. "We're not reaching anybody and I don't know why we're even trying. I don't feel like my staff is with me and our people are dead in the water. No one is willing to serve."

At least he wasn't naively optimistic!

"You didn't have *anyone* serve at your church on Sunday?" I asked Pastor "Eeyore."

"Now that you mention it, yes." He paused. "We had two new people sign up to serve in the nursery."

"And?" I asked.

"They really enjoyed serving."

"That's good to hear. And you're certain you didn't have any visitors?"

"Hang on. Let me check," he said. "Well, we did have three connection cards turned in."

I wanted to crawl through the phone and grab him by the collar (in love, of course). "Pastor, I want you to stop creating this dysfunctional culture in your church," I said. "Okay, here's your assignment for this week: Next time you talk to your spouse, your staff, your board—even your barista—I want you to say, 'Last Sunday was such a great day! God brought two, maybe three, new families. Two people signed up to serve for the first time ever. You know what? Those are the heroes of our church. That's what I love about our church!' That's how you change the beliefs and behaviors!"

Even over the phone, I could feel the energy change. Language creates culture, for good or bad. Let me say it again: Your church will become tomorrow what you celebrate (or complain about) today.

Simply put, celebrating wins is a no-brainer way to shift your beliefs and behaviors Cultural Beams. It doesn't cost you a penny and it creates an unbelievable amount of momentum—but only if you connect the wins to the Cultural DNA of the church. And don't simply celebrate wins—celebrate people as well. In every way possible, make the people in your church the heroes, not you as the pastor. Don't tell a story about when you invited someone to church. Your congregation expects that of you. Instead, tell a story about a long-time member who was terrified to invite her neighbor but did it anyway. Celebrate her and people like her.

And I know this sounds obvious, but never forget that you are ultimately celebrating God. You are celebrating that He's the One building His church. I keep repeating, "New Lifers, everything that is happening here brings glory to God and God alone."

In the next chapter, we're finally going to start talking about MCIs—that match that lights a fire under your church. "Celebrate Wins" becomes even more important in the middle of an MCI. Here's why. When a contractor is well into a renovation, the walls are down, chunks of brick are everywhere, dust fills the air, lumber is stacked in the yard, and the noise is deafening. That's what it's like midway through an MCI. During this time, people wonder if anything good will ever come out of the mess. By celebrating wins, you'll show the progress. You'll keep morale high and communicate, "We're almost there!" It's the easiest way to keep your people engaged in the middle of any initiative.

> **PRO TIP |**
> Take time to celebrate wins at the beginning of every staff and board meeting and be sure to connect them to your church's mission, values, and vision (we devote the first fifteen minutes of New Life's weekly staff chapel to this). Watch how this changes the mood in your Leadership Community.

3. Cast Vision

In Chapter 3, I talked about the difference between *having* and *casting* a vision. This is a cultural architect's most powerful tool. Understand that, simply having a vision won't change anyone's beliefs or behaviors—you have to cast it with excitement and force. You have to give your church a clear picture of tomorrow that demands action today. (You have completed the "vision narrative" in your Strategy Booklet, right?) As I said, I use aspirational language, "I see a church that…", and then paint a picture of who we can be and of the impact we'll have for God's kingdom. Then I connect the dots between this vision and our cultural voice.

In my experience, there are three steps to casting a vision:

See it.

You must see it personally before you can share it. Period. You need an actual picture to take it from theoretical to concrete, from an idea to a reality. Here are a few tips:

- Visit a church that is already doing it.
- Network with other pastors so you can ask specific questions and brainstorm.

- Draw it out. We literally have a whiteboard in every office of New Life so we can diagram to our heart's content. I also have one in my dining room. Yes, I'm a church geek.
- Study other churches' websites, but be careful. Nothing replaces seeing it in person, and just like a web dating service, online representations can be misleading.

Show it.

Once you've seen it, you need to show it. One of the most effective ways to cast vision to your Leadership Community is to literally show it to them at another church, which is why I took my key leaders to Andy Stanley's church (Chapter 2). Or, as another example, I'm currently showing them the digital upgrade I've envisioned for our next relaunch by exploring other churches' social media strategies and bringing in the people who worked on those sites.

Here are some ways to "show" your people the vision:

- Use stories of changed lives and say, "This is our vision. This is who we are."
- Draw diagrams that show people how you want your church to function.
- Give personal examples of beliefs and behaviors you want your church to exhibit.
- Use language, metaphors, and imagery to help your church see the vision.

Share it.

You've seen it and shown it, and now, you can share it. Everything you need to know about casting vision can be learned from watching *Shark Tank*. If you haven't seen it, it's a "reality TV" show where contestants have one shot at persuading venture capitalists to "buy-in" and invest in their products. The show has taught me that when I cast vision, I need to:

- Be prepared and well-rehearsed.
- Use visuals, because seeing is believing.
- Keep it short and punchy.

- Know my financial numbers.
- Answer questions quickly.
- Keep smiling.

When you cast vision, you are trying to create buy-in. You are trying to change beliefs and behaviors. Do everything you can to help your people see why they can't afford *not* to invest their time, energy, money, and heart into the vision.

Read your Vision Narrative from time to time in the church service. If you don't tear up when you read it, you need to rewrite it. Let the vision sink deep inside your heart. Every time you see, show, and share your vision, you are creating the cultural voice of your church.

> **PRO TIP |**
> Watch an episode or two of Shark Tank and observe how each contestant presents the vision of his or her product. Note the questions the panel asks and how they're answered. Write the lessons down, and use them to cast vision at your church.

4. Create a Cultural Lexicon

Every church has its specific language—words and phrases they repeat and emphasize as they talk to one another. Most of the time, it's not planned; it just evolves. But if you're intentional, you can create a cultural lexicon that reflects and reinforces the culture God is birthing in your heart. And I mean a literal lexicon—a document that outlines the cultural voice of your church and is included in your Strategy Booklet. Visit www.recalibrategroup.com/culturalvoice for a copy of New Life's Cultural Voice. It includes:

- Words and simple definitions: It's okay to have some insider language that makes it easier for you to communicate. If I say "Load-bearing Walls" or "cheese factor," my team knows what I mean.
- Stories you tell: Keep track of the key stories from the past and today that make your church what it is.
- Metaphors: Verbal pictures that are worth a thousand words, like, "The church is not a museum for saints. We're a hospital for

sinners." That's a sermon by itself! Intentionally collect and use metaphors that shape your Cultural DNA.

- Phrases and axioms: Whether borrowed from other sources or created internally, these are statements that drive "how we do things around here." For instance:
  - o Less is more.
  - o Think progress, not perfection.
  - o The main thing is to keep the main thing, the main thing.
  - o God made it. We broke it. Jesus fixed it. The church shares it.
  - o Leading change is a dance, not a war.
  - o Change isn't change until things change.
  - o Language creates culture.

Sloppy language costs you and your church dearly, but carefully crafted communication is more valuable than gold. Until you've embedded your cultural voice into the life of your church, you will never make change stick. But when you get people talking about your new culture, it will take root and produce a lot of fruit.

Transform the language, transform the culture. It's that simple.

PRO TIP |
Your cultural lexicon should be reviewed by the Leadership Community a couple times a year and it's also a great tool for on-boarding new hires. Don't, however, post online or distribute to your church—it requires too much explanation and will only confuse people.

RECALIBRATE NOW

Chapter 8: Create a Cultural Lexicon

THINK ABOUT IT!

1. Summarize the big idea of this chapter in your own words.

2. What is something new you learned?

3. What is something you disagree with or don't understand?

TALK ABOUT IT!

1. What are some specific ways you've seen that "language creates culture"?

2. On a scale of 1-5, how well are you doing at connecting your events and activities with your values? Ask the same of people from your congregation.

3. Do you lean more towards being critically pessimistic or naively optimistic? How does that affect how you communicate to your church?

4. Do you think creating a cultural lexicon is essential to your church or is it overkill?

TAKE ACTION!

Start building your cultural lexicon and add it to the Strategy Booklet—I say "start" because this can't be done in one meeting. Collect ideas, words, phrases, metaphors, and stories that describe what you want your church to become.

Meet with your Leadership Community and add more entries. Sit on your entries for a little while to make sure they ring true. You can use New Life's Cultural Voice as an example but only "copy and paste" if it resonates with you (www.Recalibrategroup.com/culturalvoice).

While your lexicon will always be a "work in progress," when you've finished this assignment, your Strategy Booklet will be complete. Congratulations! I'd love to see a copy.

Email it to me at drtroy@recalibrategroup.com.

SECTION II
THE MCI

"Define it. Date It. Do it."

—*Recalibrate Axiom*

9

The MCI Relaunch Plan

"Don't tinker with your church—Relaunch it."

—Recalibrate Axiom

In the fall of 2011, New Life was buzzing and I was, frankly, feeling very good. We'd been in our new building for eighteen months, our attendance had nearly doubled, and we'd launched our first campus. Randy McMillan, my business pastor at the time, likes to say I was at the top of my game and could have easily slid into "the Comfort Zone." I'd led the church through a massive building project, renovated our culture, and we'd recently baptized 100 people on a single Sunday! But deep inside, I already felt a new status quo setting in, so I hired a consultant to help me confront the status quo.

He walked around the church, talked to staff and members, attended our Sunday services, and did all the stuff a consultant should do. We decided to meet over dinner that evening and I walked into our meeting feeling pretty good. I knew there'd be a couple of things to improve, but we were one of the biggest churches in the Pacific Northwest. We must be doing something right, right? He sat me down and handed me a ten-page document—I didn't realize he'd have ten pages of compliments! And the first page was all the things we were doing well. The next nine pages revealed the stark truth. Your children's ministry is unfinished, your branding sucks, and the list went on.

I was stunned. I was angry. I felt stupid. Why hadn't I seen all these problems? (For the same reason you need a Realtor; no one can truly see— or smell—their own house!) The consultant's findings disheartened us, and we spent the next month going back and forth about this change and that. All the while, my holy discontent was growing. Finally, on an October morning, I woke up and said to myself, "That's it! We need to stop talking and start doing." I walked into the conference room, interrupted a meeting, gathered my strategy team, and said, "On February 12th, 2012, we *are* going to relaunch the church. We *will* launch a Saturday night service. We *will* redo the kid's ministry. We will totally rebrand New Life. All of this will be done on 'two-twelve-twelve.'"

They were a little surprised, but setting a date ignited a fire and galvanized them into shaking up the status quo. Randy was there and he says, "At that meeting, we realized we couldn't rest on our success. It shocked us into saying, 'Game on! What's next?'" The energy in the room grew and everyone was on the same page. The ideas started to flow, and we quickly developed four Rally Points, then added almost fifty High Impact Changes we wanted to make during the relaunch. Finally, we gave it a name: "2.12.12." My wife teases me because my names aren't the most creative. But "being creative" is not the most important thing—we'll get to that in the next chapter.

After that meeting, a lightbulb flipped on in my head—this is what I'd been doing for the last 25 years. As a youth pastor, a district youth director, and a lead pastor, I'd instinctively been using the power of bold initiatives. Now "2.12.12" was my first fully-formed Mission Critical Initiative: One bold initiative (relaunch the church) with a handful of Rally Points (launch Saturday service, revamp children's ministry, and update our branding) and a bunch of High Impact Changes that galvanized the church and created massive momentum. See MCI Relaunch Plan of 2.12.12 on our site at www.recaibrategroup.com/2-12-12.

Can you see how a bold Initiative will be the igniter that lights a fire under your church? It's your strategy for relaunching your established church, getting it unstuck, and recalibrating it to God's vision. It's your one domino, your moonshot. But you can also see how easily an MCI can go wrong. That's why this book started with the seven practices. I want to briefly review them, but this time showing how they relate to your MCI. Notice that they build on each other but aren't chronological steps. They need to become ongoing habits.

Practice #1: Confront the Status Quo

" *Leaders disrupt the status quo.* "

Hiring that consultant gave us both the information and the motivation we needed. If it weren't for him, we might still be comfortable with 3,000 in attendance and two campuses, instead of five campuses with over 5,000 people. Every MCI begins with the conviction that "God has more for our church."

The cultural architect carefully and honestly appraises the current reality, asking the God question, the gut question, and the gutsy question. The arsonist charges in recklessly, driven more by personal tastes or the newest church-growth trick than his church's actual needs.

Practice #2: Clarify Your Culture

" *Transform the culture, transform the church.* "

As you discover what your church's culture really is, you must determine where you want it to be. You need to sharpen your church's cultural ax and clarify her cultural DNA based upon a conviction about your mission, values, and vision. Then you need to determine which ministries are critical to your mission—focus on the ones that create or support momentum, and not derail it. Together, these four elements of the cultural ax provide the weight, momentum, direction, and focus for the edge of your MCI.

The cultural architect develops a holistic vision for the entire church, purposefully directing the renovations towards a singular mission. The arsonist runs from change to change without considering the bigger picture.

Practice #3: Trust the Story

" *Yesterday values are embers for tomorrow's vision.* "

The ax handle of your church's story allows you to wield the culture ax with precision. Established churches have a great heritage that you need to

121

discover and leverage. Some of the best MCIs are rooted in your church's past.

The cultural architect respects the past and finds ways to integrate the renovations into the church's heritage. The arsonist is in love with being on the cutting edge and arrogantly believes that new is always better. He thinks nothing of painting over a hardwood floor with this year's trendiest color.

Practice #4: Triage Changes

> 66 *Not everything needs to change overnight.* 99

Not all renovations are equal and not every change needs to be made *now*. Carefully categorize them by impact and resistance. To everything there is a time and season, and triage allows you to choose the right time for the right change.

The cultural architect knows which walls are load-bearing and which aren't, allowing him to renovate his established church without it falling down all around him. The arsonist doesn't know the difference between a Load-bearing Wall and a couch. He'll move anything he pleases and blame the resulting destruction on everything but his own stupidity.

Practice #5: Dance, Don't Fight

> 66 *Leading change is a dance, not a war.* 99

It's easy to view the "older brothers" as enemies of progress, but they are part of your flock just as much as your biggest cheerleader. Treated with respect, they may become some of your greatest allies. Learning to "leak, listen, lead, and land" not only honors them but also opens up a goldmine of wisdom and perspective. Your MCI will give you lots of chances to practice your dance moves!

The cultural architect knows how to respect and glean from dissenting voices. The arsonist only listens to his "young men" (like Rehoboam in 1 Kings 12:1-16) and treats anyone who disagrees as the enemy—which makes the real Enemy very happy.

Practice #6: Reset the Beams

> **❝** *Change isn't change until things change.* **❞** |

If an MCI doesn't begin a shift in the church's culture, then it's nothing more than hype. The key to lasting change lies in the very resistance you encountered when making the changes. Moving the Cultural Beams of budget, bandwidth, beliefs, and behaviors isn't done overnight; it requires careful, intentional, and far-sighted effort, but a well-executed MCI provides the momentum to ease the transition.

The cultural architect creates change that becomes part of the church's heritage by strategically shifting Cultural Beams. The arsonist can't understand why his church-growth tricks don't work and will probably start looking for a less "stubborn" church.

Practice #7: Make It Stick

> **❝** *Language creates culture.* **❞** |

Your most important tool for lasting change lies in changing the church's language. Language creates culture. Continual and intentional communication will move Cultural Beams and pave the way for effective MCIs.

The cultural architect connects everything back to the church's values and celebrates wins. The arsonist assumes everyone understands the "whys" and then spends his time berating his flock for their laziness.

MCI ReLAUNCH Strategy

Your Mission Critical Initiative. We're finally here. An MCI has three deceptively simple steps:

- **Define it**: What is "it"?
- **Date it**: When will you do "it"?
- **Do it**: How will you do "it"?

Together, these create your MCI Relaunch Plan, a straightforward document that will guide you as you lead your church's moonshot. Again, deceptively simple, but effective. I also call this my momentum strategy because, by setting a date, you get the thing moving and it's easier to steer a moving car than a parked one. Just about any obstacle can be conquered this way and it's become a part of how we do things at New Life. Whenever we get stuck in "analysis paralysis," someone invariably shouts, "Define it, date it, do it!" It gets a laugh out of us but forces us to stop talking and start doing.

In the rest of this section, we'll get down to the nitty-gritty. Looking back at the two types of leaders in Chapter 5, if you're a Visionary, a leap-first leader, you may be tempted to skim this. I get it. But I'd encourage you to slow down and avoid the mistakes I've made. Lean on your team members who have an eye for details.

On the other hand, maybe you're a Strategist and lean more towards discussion than action. I'm all for analysis and planning, but you have to understand that the common factor among successful leaders isn't great planning, intelligence, resources, or even experience. The common factor is *a ruthless bias toward action.*

For that reason, I want you to set what I call a "placeholder date" for your MCI now. Yes, now, even before you've defined it. That's what I'd make you do if I were coaching you. Saying, "We're going to do something by this date!" will get you off your butt and create anticipation. Think of it like this: Let's say that skydiving was on your bucket list. Which of these options is more likely to make your wish a reality?

1. Wait until you feel completely ready, then set a date.
2. Set the date, pay the fees, then get ready.

The correct answer is #2, in case you were wondering. (Imagine that I'm winking at you right now, as if to say, "I'm not being a complete jerk, but I am pretty serious about this.")

In the next three chapters, I'll walk you through creating your MCI. As I said in the Introduction, if you faithfully complete the Recalibrate NOW exercises, you *will* finish this book with your Strategy Booklet and MCI

Relaunch Plan. More importantly, you will ignite a fire in your church without burning it down.

Before we start, there are two important things to know:

1. This Is a Template, Not a Tablet

This isn't a magic spell that promises unbelievable results if every step is precisely followed. I'm always skeptical of any method that requires slavish adherence. This isn't a tablet carved into stone but a template for you to customize. It's like when I open a Word document: I may change the font, font size, margins, and headings. Take the practices in this section and adapt them for your context.

Over the years, I've learned an overriding principle: "adapt, don't adopt." Whenever you learn a new system, adapt it to your church's context, its current realities, your leadership style, and the strengths and weaknesses of your entire team. Treating this as a tablet will paralyze you. Using it as a template will spark creativity and life into you and your Leadership Community.

I was recently working with a pastor who was eager to get his church unstuck, but I kept running into a roadblock whenever I asked him to date his relaunch. I started wondering if his heart was really in it. When the breakthrough happened, it had nothing to do with willingness.

"I just don't like that word 'relaunch,'" he said. It wasn't just him—it was throwing off his board members as well.

"Then don't use it! It works for us, but let's customize it for your church," I said. "You keep talking about hope. How about 'The Hope Initiative'?"

His eyes lit up and he said, "We can do that? Well, here's our Bold Idea: On October 4, 2020, our church is launching the HOPE initiative."

2. The Importance of Launch Energy

Think of the energy it takes to launch a rocket or for a plane to take off—20% of its fuel by some estimates. The same is true of a Mission Critical Initiative. For it to succeed, you must be emotionally, mentally, and spiritually prepared to devote 20% of your time, energy, and focus. So, if you work fifty hours a week, then you must invest ten of those hours into your MCI. This is even more true for bi-vocational pastors. If you're only able to commit twenty hours a week to your church, four of those need to be dedicated to your MCI. This is a huge investment, no doubt. But New Life is the church she is because of the 20% I've invested in our MCIs, not the 80% spent in everyday duties. Besides, maintaining the status quo already requires massive amounts of your bandwidth—why not spend it instead on something that will ignite your church?

I'm going to shoot straight: if you aren't willing to devote 20% of your bandwidth to your MCI, then don't expect the results I've talked about. But if you are, then expect a huge payoff in a relatively short period of time. Look, I get that life happens. There have been times that I couldn't give a full 20%—and I've always felt the difference. We still see good results, but not like we're used to.

So where can you find that 20%? Here are some ways I've discovered to get more bandwidth:

- Learn the fine art of saying "no."
- Share the pastoral role.
- Develop a teaching team and preach less (the weeks I don't preach aren't vacations—they're when I make the most "forward progress"!).
- Staff to your weaknesses.
- Don't neglect your health.
- Counterintuitively: Take summer breaks and personal retreats.

By the way, this 20% launch energy applies to your entire MCI Relaunch team (more on that in Chapter 12). If there are three of you working fifty hours a week, that's thirty hours targeted to kick-starting your church's momentum.

RECALIBRATE NOW

Chapter 9: Set the Placeholder Date

THINK ABOUT IT!

1. Summarize the big idea of this chapter in your own words.
2. What is something new you learned?
3. What is something you disagree with or don't understand?

TALK ABOUT IT!

1. Which one of the practices are you currently doing the best? Which needs the most improvement?
2. In the past, have you treated church-growth programs more like tablets or templates?
3. How can you and your staff allocate 20% of your bandwidth to the MCI?
4. Will your MCI relaunch your church or a specific ministry?

TAKE ACTION!

By now, you probably have a "30,000-foot view" of Mission Critical Initiatives. Get away from the office and prayerfully review the Strategy Booklet and your answers to the "God, Gut, and Gutsy Questions." With the Holy Spirit's direction and using everything you've learned, ask, "What is my moonshot? My domino?"

Trim down your list to two-three big ideas and be ready to leak them to your Leadership Community and key influencers (Chapter 6). You're looking for responses that say, "Oh wow, if we could pull that off..."

With all that, and a rough idea of how much work you have ahead, set a placeholder date (to be finalized in Chapter 11) and share it with your Leadership Community.

10

DEFINE IT:
WHAT IS "IT"?

"Be clear, not clever."

—Recalibrate Axiom

On December 14, 2004, Dr. Don Berwick, CEO of the Institute for Healthcare Improvement, stood before a room full of hospital administrators as they faced an upsetting reality: thousands upon thousands of patients were dying every year due to preventable mistakes. Not giving the post-surgical antibiotics at the right time. Failure to properly prepare the patient for surgery. Improper management of ventilators.

In the past, the Institute had laid out a great plan for specific, research-driven procedures that could save lives, but they were only a non-profit organization with no power to enforce these changes. To make it worse, liability issues made hospitals reluctant to admit that there was a problem. Dr. Berwick didn't have any authority over these administrators—all he had was influence (sound familiar?).

After reminding everyone of the problem (Chapter 2), he said, "Here is what I think we should do. I think we should save 100,000 lives. And I think we should do that by June 14, 2006—18 months from today." He paused. "By 9:00 A.M."

Now that's an MCI! He practically wanted to relaunch the entire health care system. Notice the clarity: "Save 100,000 lives by June 14, 2006, 9:00 A.M." Known as "The 100,000 Lives Campaign," this crystal-clear moonshot was backed up by specific strategies for training hundreds of thousands of

129

healthcare workers. And it worked. Perhaps millions of lives have been saved by the ongoing effects of this initiative.

It may not have been the cleverest-sounding plan, but it was clear. That is the sort of clarity you need to bring to your MCI when you define it.

Clarity is king.

Your Domino

As a quick reminder, your Mission Critical Initiative is that first domino that creates the momentum to knock your church out of its status quo. As I said in Chapter 1, a domino can knock over something 50% bigger than itself. That is the power of momentum.

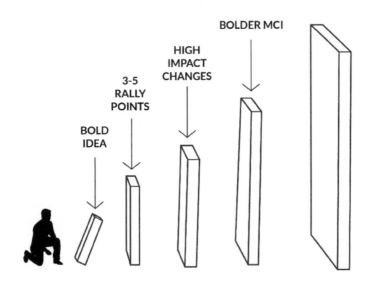

Four Essentials of an MCI Relaunch Plan

In case you haven't already noticed, I believe in the power of writing things down. Just like setting a date, it solidifies your plans and creates accountability. An MCI Relaunch Plan is simply getting all the key points of your MCI on one page (you can download a template at www.recalibrategroup.com/MCIRelaunchplan). You can also see four examples there, including ones from each of the pastors in the Recalibrate Profiles. Your MCI Relaunch Plan has four essential elements:

- The Father's Heart.
- One Bold Idea.
- 3-5 big Rally Points.
- High Impact Changes.

Essential #1: The Father's Heart

The pastor in the diagram is kneeling, symbolic of the wisdom, humility, and servanthood needed to renovate a church. You need the Father's heart towards the younger and older brother, reaching the lost sinner and honoring the church pillar. Guard against selfish ambition, keep repenting, and submit yourself to God and godly counsel, or else you'll end up burning your whole church down. The list of torched churches is depressingly long.

Okay, altar call's over.

Essential #2: One Bold Idea

If you've been walking through the seven practices and their "Recalibrate NOWs," then you should already have a pretty good idea of the changes that need to happen in your church. It's probably an anxiety-inducing long list. It's time to narrow it down to one Bold Idea that relaunches your church or a ministry, or launches a new ministry. Remember, you don't have to do everything at once. You're looking for a single, bold initiative that unites your church around the one thing that will make the single greatest impact now. You'll accomplish much more than that, but only one idea can be at the core, for example:

- John F. Kennedy: "I believe that this nation should commit itself to achieving the goal, before this decade is out, of landing a man on the moon and returning him safely to Earth."

- Dr. Don Berwick: "I think we should save 100,000 lives. I think we should do that by June 14, 2006. By 9:00 A.M."

Not only are they bold, but they're expressed in unforgettable statements that engage people's hearts. You need to create a similar Bold Idea. But it doesn't need to be complicated. Try using this format:

"WHO will do WHAT by WHEN."

It's clear, simple, and complete. Once you've done that, you can play with the words and the order. This was New Life's Bold Idea for the 2.12.12 initiative:

"On February, 12th 2012 [WHEN], we [WHO] are going to relaunch the church [WHAT]."

Something like this seems simple to say, but it's huge. Speaking your Bold Idea out loud (that's key) turns it into a commitment. It will engage emotions, create conviction, and begin a chain reaction.

One more point: notice the "we" —this isn't your personal project. Everyone in the Leadership Community owns the bold Initiative, everyone sets aside their own agendas for the sake of the moonshot. No ministry gets to sit this one out.

PRO TIP |
Less is more. You might follow the "Twitter rule" and keep it to 280 characters or less. JFK's statement was 160 characters.

Now you need to give your Bold Idea a name. As I write this, my editor, my publisher, and I are going back and forth on the title of this book because we know that can be a "make or break" thing. You want to be intentional about your MCI name. People will rally around and remember it for years. Think of Dr. Don Berwick's name: "The 100,000 Lives Campaign." Simple but compelling—I'm ready for action! You want your name to:

- Be memorable.
- Spark interest.
- Create a buzz.
- Be brief and simple to say (you're going to use it a hundred times, so don't choose a tongue twister!).

Here's what works for me. Grab some of your most creative people and brainstorm. Throw around the craziest ideas you can think of because they're far more inspiring than sensible ones. Here are the MCI names from the Recalibrate Profiles you've been reading:

- Everyday Heroes
- To Be the Church
- NOW Initiative
- Awakening Initiative
- 2.12.12

Essential #3: Define 3-5 Rally Points

I'm not talking about "goals." In my experience, goals de-energize people. You need to *rally* your Leadership Community and congregation behind specific objectives. Hence "rally points"— the tangible results of your MCI. Said another way, if your Bold Idea says, "WHO will do WHAT by WHEN," then your Rally Points say "HOW."

They will typically be Q2: Graceful Dance changes—high impact, high resistance. If it's low impact, it shouldn't be part of your Initiative. If it's low resistance, you probably don't need an MCI to pull it off. Through trial and error, I've discovered that three to five is the magic number for Rally Points. Two is underwhelming and more than five is overwhelming!

Each of the Rally Points must be anchored in your Bold Idea. Accordingly, MCIs that relaunch the *entire church* should have Rally Points based on your MCMs. MCIs that focus on a *specific ministry* should have Rally Points based on that ministry. For example, you wouldn't want "more people in groups" as a rally point for a "relaunch kids' ministry" MCI. But New Life's 2.12.12 MCI was a relaunch of the entire church, so its Rally Points related to our MCMs:

1) Launch a new Saturday Service with 500 people.
2) Relaunch Kids' Ministry with 800 kids.
3) Launch a new gathering at the Maple Valley Campus.
4) Relaunch our website & branding.

Notice that these are "clear, not clever." No fancy wording. I'll get creative later, when I cast the vision.

You and your Leadership Community need to choose the three to five most impactful Rally Points that spring from your Bold Idea. Begin by going through all your changes from Chapter 5 and make a list of all the ones that relate to your one "Bold Idea." Use those to kickstart a brainstorming session. Once you have a list of several possible Rally Points, prayerfully consider your options and ask if they pass the "MCI Litmus Test."

The short version of my litmus test is: "Does it get the blood pumping in my Leadership Community?" If not, I go back to the drawing board. But if it passes that, we then use this longer version to examine each rally point, one by one:

a) Is It Bold and Believable?

This is the fine line of leadership: If your Rally Points aren't bold, your church won't sit on the edge of their seats in anticipation. They'll sit back and let someone else do it. But if they aren't believable, they'll write you off and you'll lose credibility. Here's how I help churches walk that line. I ask the Leadership Community (not the pastor), "Do you believe your church can do this?" Then, "Does this rally point stretch you?"

> **PRO TIP |**
> Your team may struggle to be completely honest with you—either because you're their boss or their friend. You may want to bring someone in from the outside.

b) Is It New, Newish, or New to You?

Momentum, by its very nature, is created when something is new. But *new* doesn't necessarily mean *brand new*. Sometimes, your goal is "simply" to refresh a ministry so that it feels new! Here are three different types of new:

- New: Something your church hasn't ever done before.

- Newish: Something that's been done but has lost its passion and conviction. Something that needs a fresh vision and fresh ideas. For example, New Life had a strong mission focus in the past, but we needed a new plan, approach, and burden for missions. So, we relaunched missions as Kingdom Builders. It's an old idea but feels brand new—and you won't believe the energy it's created!

- New to you: Something your church did before you got there and now you get to recalibrate it.

c) Is It Clear, Concise, and Concrete?

Which one of these Rally Points would you prefer to say ten times in a sermon? "Our church is about community and discipleship, and therefore we want our people to form more discipleship groups and start sharing life with each other and then we'll eventually have a lot of groups."

Or, "Develop twenty new life groups by Feb 12, 2012."

Make your Rally Points clear. Keep them short. Choose concrete action words over philosophical concepts. And please don't try to be too clever! There's a place for creative language, but you don't want to sacrifice clarity to creativity.

d) Is It Measurable?

Notice that all of the 2.12.12 Rally Points have very clear objectives. Two of them have specific numbers. There needs to be a way to know if we won. Vague metrics are safe. Clarity is bold. Guess which one creates momentum?

The Rally Points are your scoreboard. How do you keep score of "We want to help feed the hungry of the world"? You can't. But how about: "On September 15, we'll launch a weekly program to provide food boxes for 300 people in Northbrook Apartment complex." That's a score your congregation will want to track—and contribute to. Requiring your MCI to be measurable forces your Leadership Community to transition from theoretical to concrete. By the way, this test can also be applied to your "High Impact Changes" (the next MCI essential element).

"But what if we don't hit our Rally Points?" That's one of the first things pastors ask. I can't say this enough—your goal isn't reaching a goal. It's about momentum, not metrics. Metrics provide the "bold but believable," but if your Rally Points galvanize people, if they inspire your church and move it forward, if they get your congregation praying, stretching, and believing in God, then you've won. By all means, try to meet or even exceed your goals, but you won't lose credibility if you miss a metric but gain momentum. Don't get discouraged, celebrate moving the ball forward.

Essential #4: High Impact Changes

High Impact Changes ride the momentum of your Mission Critical Initiative to accomplish more in your church than you thought possible. This is the platform to make as many mission critical changes as your budget and bandwidth allows. Win! Win! Win! That is your goal with High Impact Changes.

Think of your MCI's momentum like a perfect surfing wave, developing off of Oahu's North Shore. Does the wave care how many surfers ride it all the way home? Not at all! Load as many High Impact Changes on that baby as possible. My business pastor jokingly says that relaunching the church gives him an excuse to make unsexy changes. You might find your administrator getting excited about things like a new database, upgraded financial systems, and payroll management. Anything that is critical to move your mission forward.

Don Ross, Network Leader of the Assemblies of God Northwest Ministry Network, relaunched his church with an MCI and said, "The genius behind an MCI is that it allows you to change 40 or 50 things simultaneously."

Is it possible to add too many High Impact Changes into your MCI Relaunch Plan? Technically, yes. Too many surfers riding on a wave will start banging into each other. You don't want them to detract from the Rally Points nor overtax your budget and bandwidth. But in reality, no. Almost every church I've coached makes the mistake of choosing too few, not too many, High Impact Changes.

First, look at your Rally Points and brainstorm as many related High Impact Changes as possible. As with any brainstorming session, kick the word "realistic" out the window. Go crazy now and edit later. Second, go back to all the "cringe factors" from your one-day offsite. It doesn't matter whether or not they relate to the Rally Points, just add them to the list! Check out the MCI Relaunch Plans on https://recalibrategroup.com/MCIRelaunchplan and notice how their High Impact Changes include things that are, and are not, related to their Rally Point. Third, organize the High Impact Changes into categories to keep them from becoming overwhelming. The number of categories is 100% your call—I don't even have a rule of thumb (Jana will tell you how rare that is!).

Not only does creating this list provide you with a multitude of wins, but it also creates a culture of change. Like JFK's moonshot, which brought many unexpected advances in everything from car engineering to food processing, you can't anticipate the impact of your MCI. Do it right and you'll have a cascade of changes, planned and unplanned!

Crummy First Drafts

At this point, you have all the information you need to start planning your MCI. In the "Recalibrate NOW" section of this chapter and the next, you'll complete your MCI Relaunch Plan. But first, I want to give you an important tip: Don't overthink this.

My editor likes to talk about the "Crummy First Draft Principle" of writing (it's actually called something else, but that's close enough): The first draft is always crummy and if you aren't okay with crummy writing, you'll never write anything good because the magic happens in the editing.

Likewise, just drafting an MCI Relaunch Plan (and setting a date!) is half the battle. Don't get bogged down in the details. Dream big now and narrow your focus later. And don't be afraid to tweak things as you go. It's a tablet, not the Ten Commandments. Work with your team and pivot when necessary.

Okay, we've defined your MCI Relaunch Plan—time to date it!

RECALIBRATE NOW

Chapter 10: Write the MCI Relaunch

THINK ABOUT IT!

1. Summarize the big idea of this chapter in your own words.

2. What is something new you learned?

3. What is something you disagree with or don't understand?

TALK ABOUT IT!

1. What is the role of eager and expectant faith in building your MCI?

2. Why is it crucial that your Rally Points be both bold and believable?

3. What makes the High Impact Changes the "genius" of an MCI?

4. Why do you need to start with a "crummy first draft"?

TAKE ACTION!

Now, it's time for the first draft of your MCI Relaunch Plan. Use the template from www.recalibrategroup.com/MCIRelaunchplan, but remember that it is just a template, not a tablet. Work with your Leadership Community and use your Strategy Booklet to:

1. Craft your One Bold Idea: *"WHO will do WHAT by WHEN."*

2. Choose the name.

3. Decide on three to five Rally Points.

4. Brainstorm many High Impact Changes.

That's it—you've just planned your first MCI! Okay, I wish it was that easy, but you're off to a strong start.

11

DATE IT:
WHEN WILL YOU DO "IT"?

"Dreams without deadlines are dead ends."

—Recalibrate Axiom

Four years after we relaunched New Life with our 2.12.12 initiative, we relaunched it again with a bolder MCI, called 3.16.16. This MCI had four Rally Points: 1) Empower 100 deacons, 2) Launch a new ministry, Kingdom Builders, 3) Do 316 service projects in 30 days, and 4) Launch a new vision for our campuses—our slogan was "One Church...Five Campuses."

When we launched the MCI at a "vision night," the room was packed and the energy was high as I walked the church through the four Rally Points and the High Impact Changes we had in store. Did I say, "walked through?" No, I painted a picture and casted a vision. On the wall was a huge map of the Seattle area with our three current campuses clearly displayed.

I pointed to Kent, the location for our upcoming campus and then, in the excitement of the night and (I believe) under the inspiration of the Holy Spirit, I went off-script.

"Kent, a city with 139 languages. The most diverse city in Washington. A city that needs Jesus. A city that Jesus loves. Why not plant a church of 1,000 people in Kent? That's our BOLD initiative, a church of 1,000 people in Kent by this time next year."

As soon as I said it, I realized how crazy it was. Definitely bold, but was it believable? I saw Pastor Randy shaking his head in the front pew. When I sat down, Jana whispered to me, "What were you thinking?"

"I don't know!" I was scared to death.

The boldness of the vision inspired the church, but it was the date that galvanized the staff. We didn't have until "someday" to reach this goal. We had twelve months. Long story short, New Life Kent became a healthy church of 800 people. Not quite 1,000 but no one who was there that night is complaining.

The Power of a D.A.T.E.

As the Recalibrate axiom says, "Dreams without deadlines are dead ends." Period. Every discouraged pastor dreams about getting unstuck. They read all the books, attend conferences, and have endless meetings. But like too many engaged couples, they wait until they feel completely ready to set a date. (Hint: You'll never feel completely ready.)

As you'll remember, I asked you to set a placeholder date. When I consult with a church, we first set a date and *then* create the MCI Relaunch Plan. In fact, if they aren't willing to set a date, I won't work with them. It's that serious. Without a date, I'd put my money on your MCI never happening. Setting a date changes everything: there's more excitement, more creativity, and more engagement by the Leadership Community. Suddenly, everyone is paying attention to the details and engaging their brain.

Four crucial and practical things happen when you and your Leadership Community set a date. Using the acronym D.A.T.E., it:

...defines the scope: The moment the date is set, the "scope" of your MCI will be clearly defined. Smaller ones take less time, bigger ones take more. You and your team can start asking "Can we get this done by this date?" You may even need to adjust some of your Rally Points and save some of your High Impact Changes for the next MCI. Or maybe you'll want to adjust the date—that's the nice thing about setting a placeholder date. You get the motivation of a deadline but still have some flexibility.

...aligns people: When you set the launch date you will quickly find out if everyone is on the same page. Notice I said *alignment*, not *agreement*. Many pastors get caught in the "agreement" trap—they want total agreement before moving forward. Setting a date says, "We're doing this. Discussion's over. Now, do you want to be on board?" That to say, a specific date turns conversations into action and aligns your team in a way very few things can. At the same time, don't forget "leak, listen, lead, and land" from Chapter 6. Your Leadership Community may have suggestions you need to listen to and learn from.

...triggers momentum: Walt Disney liked to say, "Everyone needs deadlines. Even the beavers. They loaf around all summer, but when they are faced with the winter deadline, they work like fury. If we didn't have deadlines, we'd stagnate." Likewise, the authors of *Influencer* talk about the immediate power of a deadline: "The effect of providing this clear, compelling, and time-bound target was immediate. It started a whole chain of events that virtually redefined the organization."[5] The moment I said, "On February 12th, 2012, we're relaunching the church," the clock began ticking. It's like announcing a pregnancy. Something has been set in motion that can't be postponed. Setting the date will kickstart momentum in a way that you have to see to believe.

...evokes emotions: I mentioned skydiving in Chapter 9 when I told you to set a placeholder date. Let's say we were at a party together and you casually mentioned that skydiving was on your bucket list. What if I called you up the following morning and said, "I just scheduled our skydive—next Saturday, 11:00 am. I've already paid and it's non-refundable. You're welcome."

Did your pulse just spike?

Setting a clear date doesn't just affect the mind, it affects the heart. Again, from *Influencers*: "Research reveals that a clear, compelling, and challenging goal causes the blood to pump more rapidly, the brain to fire, and the muscles to engage. However, when goals are vague, no such effects take place."[6]

---

[5] Joseph Grenny, et al., *Influencer: The New Science of Leading Change* (New York: McGraw-Hill, 2013), p. 19

[6] Joseph Grenny, et al., *Influencer: The New Science of Leading Change* (New York: McGraw-Hill, 2013), p. 18

Lastly, if your church or Leadership Community has grown apathetic, setting a concrete date may be just the thing to stir hearts and restore excitement. I've seen it happen time and time again.

Steps to Setting the Official Date

So far, you've been working from a placeholder date. So, how do you turn it into an official date? Getting that right is crucial and there are several practical things to consider.

First, let's clarify what we're dating. The MCI date can be:

a) The deadline for achieving your Rally Points and High Impact Changes,

b) The date you launch something, or

c) A mixture of deadlines and launch dates.

For example, Dr. Berwick set a *deadline* (6/14/2006) for saving 100,000 people, but with New Life's "2.12.12" MCI, the date marked when we would *relaunch* our church and launch our Saturday night service. And I'm currently working with a church whose MCI Launch date is when they'll launch a remodel of their children's ministry, but also the deadline for having 500 people in small groups.

With that understood, here are seven steps I use to set the dates of our MCIs:

1. Determine the Length

The length of an MCI is directly tied to its scope. Don't belabor a simple MCI and don't rush a complex one. Here are some lengths I recommend:

- Forty days: Perfect for special emphases or campaigns (like "Forty Days of Prayer").

- Ninety Days: It takes three to six months if you're relaunching a ministry or department. Ninety days also works well to relaunch a ministry. Some of the ninety-day MCIs at New Life have focused on children's and youth ministry, Life Groups, worship, First Impressions, and Assimilation.

- Nine Months: It takes six to nine months if you're relaunching your entire church and making major Load-bearing Wall changes. As I've already said, those require skill and patience. But don't drag it out too long—most churches lose focus and passion after nine months.
- Two to Three Years: A building campaign or a new campus could take this long, as can the relaunch of a large organization, such as a denomination or university.

2. Consider the Calendar

The longer you work in a church, the easier it is to forget about the practical realities that can impact your MCI:

- School schedules, including breaks and special events (and don't forget that different districts have different dates).
- Weather.
- Daylight savings time—there's nothing worse than pouring all your energy into a big fundraiser and discovering it lands on "spring forward." Ask me how I know...
- Holidays and the natural rhythms of the year.
- Professional sports team schedules. Did someone say Seahawks game?

When you're looking at the calendar, also pay attention to the forty days before your launch date. These are frequently the "home stretch" and you don't want to be competing with the holidays for your church's attention (more on this in the next chapter). Over the years, I've collected three favorite MCI dates:

- Sunday after Super Bowl: (second Sunday in February) This gives me all of January to ramp up and allows for plenty of time before Easter. Additionally, our attendance is typically higher in February, March, and April.
- March: Same reasons as above, plus I can tie it into Easter.
- Late September/early October: Kids are back in school and everyone's in a "get back to work" mindset.

145

3. Pay Attention to the "Cultural Beams"

In Chapter 7, we talked about the Cultural Beams and how they create resistance but can also make changes stick. The more your MCI involves resetting beams, the more time you need to give it.

- Budget: If it's going to cost money and require fundraising, be sure to take timing into account—you don't want a fundraiser campaign that coincides with Christmas's credit card bills.

- Bandwidth: Pay attention to the demands on both your staff and your congregation. Again, the holidays are a really bad time for an MCI.

- Beliefs and behaviors: If your MCI is going to mess with people's beliefs and behaviors, be sure your plan includes time to teach and vision cast (Chapters 3 and 8).

4. Declare Your Launch Day

It's time to take the plunge and turn your placeholder into a concrete date. Declare it out loud to your Leadership Community and get a countdown clock that counts down to Launch Day. Up until this point, it's been a little theoretical. Now, it gets very practical. It's like the difference between saying, "We're getting married this spring," and "We're getting married on May 22nd." Time to rent the church, call the pastor, and print the invitations!

> **PRO TIP |**
> Put your countdown clock in the church's office where everyone will see it. Give them a daily reminder that, "We're relaunching in 77 days!"

5. Create the Timeline

Now, create a timeline. What are the big calendar items that need to be scheduled? Maybe planning isn't your thing. Grab some logistically-gifted people and reverse engineer a timeline of everything that needs to happen and when. By the way, this is when you'll be glad you set a date. Without it, your MCI could die at the hand of a thousand nuances.

This timeline needs to outline specific dates and critical events. Carefully think through the sequences—things must happen in the right order to be

146

successful. For example, if you were to publicly announce, "We're relaunching the church in six months!" before talking to your board...well, that would be bad. You can create it with something as simple as Word or Excel or use a professional project management program, like ASANA or Basecamp. Whatever tool you use, be sure to include the following dates:

- Mile Markers—benchmarks to ensure you're on track (see below).
- Special sermon series before or after the launch.
- A time for a prayer focus.
- The forty days before your launch Sunday.
- Launch Day. This is the big date!

Regarding "Mile Markers": These are key moments and events that ensure you're on schedule. For example, if launching a new Saturday service is one of your Rally Points, your first mile marker may be a barbecue with the Saturday night leadership team at your home. Your next marker could be a private rehearsal. Your third could be a preview service. They're "putting the hand to the plow" type moments that build momentum and measure your progress.

Once the timeline is done, you can revisit the actual date. Does it still work or does it need to be adjusted? Would it be wise to move it a week or two? For instance, if the Seattle Seahawks are having a good season and we realize I chose a playoff Sunday, we reschedule. (I've had to do this twice— Seattle is a football town.)

6. Publicly Announce the Launch Day

Up to this point, everything has been mostly internal. It may not exactly be a state secret, but you haven't taken it public and still have a little wiggle room. Now, it's time to publicly announce it to the church. You don't necessarily need to call it a relaunch or MCI. Use whatever name you gave it in Chapter 10.

In your church's eyes, this is effectively when the MCI begins and it dramatically raises the stakes. Once you announce, "On this date, we will relaunch our church," your credibility is on the line. No pressure. Actually, lots of pressure. Pressure that will drive you to prayer! Pressure that will cause you to lead again, dream again, and believe God to ignite a fire in your church.

7.   Schedule Your Next, BOLDER MCI

We'll come back to this in Chapter 13, but penciling in my next MCI allows me to dovetail it with the current one.

RECALIBRATE PROFILE: PAUL GOTTLIEB
Harvest Community Church (Roseville, CA)
Part 2

Within a month of my coming to Harvest, attendance doubled and people had to sit in the lobby! But the children's ministry was sketchy, we had no greeters, and only a single usher who'd been doing it alone for two years.

I learned a lot at the Recalibrate event and wanted to apply the principles Troy was teaching. When I met with him and explained our situation, I told him we needed to start a second service. He responded, "Don't just add a service. Relaunch your church."

I realized that he was talking about a new way of thinking, a new way of planning, a new way of leading a church. First, we had to figure out which ministries were Mission Critical. That wasn't hard because there were so few ministries! Sunday morning was the biggest Mission Critical Ministry—by far. Next, I needed to set a launch date.

It was the date that changed the game; it forced us to get serious and count the cost. The moment I said it out loud, the plan for our MCI came together. We called it the "NOW Initiative." Our theme was John 4:35, "When you plant, you always say, 'Four more months to wait before we gather the grain.' But I tell you, open your eyes, and look at the fields. They are ready for harvesting now." and 2 Corinthians 6:2, "I tell you, now is the time of God's favor, now is the day of salvation."

In the middle of all this, our youth pastor and children's pastors resigned for different reasons—and we still didn't have a full-time worship leader. Then, our bookkeeper fell and broke her ankle. I felt overwhelmed and told Troy, "We just can't pull this off. You talk about needing bandwidth, and I don't have any left!" He listened and was kind but said, "You still have to. The church needs you and it needs to be relaunched or it will stagnate. Don't let the enemy distract you from the dream!"

By God's grace, we relaunched the church on September 22, 2019. The second service was a big success. Enthusiasm was infectious, attendance went up, volunteers were excited to serve, and giving was much higher than before. One of the unexpected results was that a second service allowed more people to volunteer. Before, they hadn't wanted to miss worship, but now they could serve during one service and attend the other!

RECALIBRATE NOW

Chapter 11: Turn the Placeholder into a Concrete Date

THINK ABOUT IT!

1. Summarize the big idea of this chapter in your own words.

2. What is something new you learned?

3. What is something you disagree with or don't understand?

TALK ABOUT IT!

1. Why is it so important to set a date?

2. Will your MCI date be a launching date, a deadline, or a mixture of the two?

3. Are you good at planning things out or do you need a detail-orientated person working with you?

TAKE ACTION!

Do I have to say it? It's time to "date it." Turn that placeholder into a concrete date. You may want to even start drafting up a timeline, which you'll finalize in the next "Recalibrate NOW."

12

DO IT:
HOW WILL YOU DO "IT"?

"Stop dreaming, start doing."

—Recalibrate Axiom

I love lifting the arms of pastors. I've known discouragement and hopelessness; I've experienced the power of the right council at the right time. As a coach, I have the honor of being the one to give that council. My coaching calls usually begin with all the normal problems: My staff is stuck. My church isn't growing. I can't seem to get the congregation to reach their friends. I'll let them talk for a little bit, then say, "I have a crazy idea—let's relaunch the entire church."

There's a stunned pause on the other side. Then I say, "I'm serious. Let's redo your buildings, update your kids' ministry, remodel your lobby, rewrite your mission, values, and vision narrative. While we're at it, let's do all of those other things you've been dreaming of."

The longer we talk, the more excited they get. Until I ask, "What day are you going to 'Do it'?"

Pastors are great at saying things (aren't we?), but, as Benjamin Franklin said, "Well done is better than well said." Far, far more MCIs die because the pastor and staff simply didn't "do it," than because the church resisted change. You can walk through the seven practices, define your MCI, then date it, but without action, hard work, and diligent follow-through, nothing will happen. At some point you have to stop dreaming and start doing.

Enough talk. Let's get going!

What follows are seven vital action points. If you are a strategic leader, you'll love this chapter. But if you're more of a visionary, you might be tempted to skip it. Don't! Or, at a minimum, give it to someone you'll listen to.

ACTION POINT #1:
BUILD YOUR MCI RELAUNCH TEAM

You need to build your own "dream team." This team will be essential to your MCI's success. Everyone on the team (which includes all your key staff) needs to be fully committed, able to work together, yet able to own a specific part of the MCI. The lead pastor's job is to champion the overall MCI Relaunch Plan; therefore, you'll need someone with killer administrative skills to be the project manager and work directly with them. When you're building your MCI team, don't limit it to paid staff. Look at your key volunteers and board members. Or maybe there's already a professional project manager in your congregation and this is God's way of bringing them on board! It should include both *influencers* (those with the authority and credibility to get others on board) and *implementers* (those who follow through and get things done).

As I said, everyone needs to be able to work together while owning a specific part of the MCI. Each team member (paid or volunteer) should be given total ownership of:

1) A rally point,

2) A high impact change, or

3) Something that supports #1 or 2.

That is to say, no one gets to just talk. If they're on the team, they need to be capable of taking over some element of the MCI.

In my experience, load-bearing changes should be led by one of the executive pastors or someone with skill, influence, and credibility. But Q1: Rapid Wins can and should be delegated to an associate, board member, or even an emerging leader. It's a great way for them to gain credibility. One way to give everyone total ownership is to divide portions of a Rally Point between the key staff. For example, I was recently consulting with a church that had a Rally Point of "500 people in small groups by October 25, 2020." I encouraged them to give their youth ministry the Rally Point of "100 students in small groups" and their kids ministry "100 kids in small groups."

A note for multi-site churches: Each campus needs to be pursuing the same MCI and Rally Points, even if the metrics and specifics vary. Their High Impact Changes may differ, however.

Another important point: Even though not everyone on your staff needs to be on the MCI team (Bob the accountant might not be a "fit"), everyone—from the assistant janitor to the executive pastor—needs to be committed to it. No one gets to "sit this one out" because it isn't their department. In fact, MCIs are a powerful way to unify your team. People often ask me, "Why does the New Life team work together so well?" The short answer is "Our MCIs." At least once every year, we all work together to relaunch a ministry. Then, every three to five years, we come together to relaunch the entire church. This practice unites us and saves us from turf wars and silo building.

> **PRO TIP |**
> MCIs make great silo-crashers! Put in the extra effort to strategize ways to get different departments working together.

ACTION POINT #2:
MAKE DAILY PROGRESS

This is, by far, the most important part of making your MCI successful. Make progress every day. Remember the 20% launch energy from Chapter 9? This is where that 20% gets used. Everyone on the MCI team needs to commit to making daily progress during the MCI.

Daily progress requires focusing your bandwidth. The first thing I ask myself every morning is, "What can I do today that will have the greatest impact on moving the ball forward? What do I need to ignore today so I can see tangible results?" Catch that? *Today*, not tomorrow!

Some of the tasks I put at the top of my daily list are:

- Fine-tuning Launch Day.

- Checking in with one or two team members.
- Talking to an influential person in the church.
- Resetting a Cultural Beam (Chapter 7).
- Crafting ways to connect the dots, celebrate wins, cast vision, and create a cultural language (Chapter 8).
- Research other churches who are already doing what I want to do.
- Reading a book or listening to a podcast that spawns more ideas.

I expect this same level of focus from my entire MCI Relaunch Team. You'll be amazed by how a little daily progress can create massive momentum over ninety days, let alone nine months.

> **PRO TIP |**
> Every morning of an MCI, write down two or three things you can do that day to move it forward.

ACTION POINT #3:
PRIORITIZE WEEKLY ACCOUNTABILITY

Once a week, bring the entire MCI Relaunch team together for 35-45 minutes to touch bases, cheer each other on, and create accountability. Take this time to make assignments, fire up the troops, and review the timeline, Rally Points, and High Impact changes. I ask them two questions that are similar to the ones I ask myself every morning:

- What did you do last week that made the greatest impact on our MCI?
- What will you do this week to have the greatest impact?

> **PRO TIP |**
> Keep these meetings separate from your regular staff meetings, even if that means just taking a quick break and then saying, "Now we're in our MCI Meeting." Have someone take notes and send out action items (with due dates!) afterward.

ACTION POINT #4:

COMMUNICATE LIKE A CHURCH PLANTER

Your MCI will live or die by communication. You want to create anticipation, excitement, and the overall sense that something new is happening. Think like a church planter whose job depends on everyone showing up and is eager to grab the attention of his or her community. Here are some ways to communicate.

- Utilize social media (Twitter, Facebook, Instagram . . . and dare I suggest TikTok?).
- Create videos that share the vision and tell stories.
- Use creative signage and branding.
- Send a "Save the Date" notice three months ahead of time.
- Launch an email campaign.
- Update your website and app.
- Have every department build excitement within their ranks.

ACTION POINT #5:

RAISE THE FUNDS

Every MCI costs money; that's one reason they face resistance. Some don't require a lot of funds, but you still need to invest something to get the greatest payoff. Others can be very expensive.

When a pastor says, "We can't afford to do this!", I immediately respond, "You can't afford not to!" Your moonshot will generate excitement and generosity. People give to vision and organizations that win. And don't forget to factor in the high cost of stagnation and decline. If you don't pull the trigger and invest the money now, doing nothing will cost you far more in the long run.

This book isn't about stewardship or fundraising, but if your MCI costs are creating some concern, let me give you some overarching principles:

First, put MCIs into your budget. Don't wait to have a specific one in mind—plan to have some bold new initiative every year! Make it part of your Cultural DNA.

Second, think of it like a building campaign. Just as you raise money to fund a new building or major project, you can raise money for an MCI. We often use a staged strategy. I start by meeting with our top givers and influencers. After they're on board, we have a special offering for the MCI. People respond generously to a bold vision, so don't be shy about thinking big, planning big, and asking big.

Finally, learn to be extremely strategic with your funds. We might temporarily shift some finances from other ministries to fund the MCI. We brainstorm ways to get the most bang for our buck—I've discovered that limited resources force us to think outside the box. Scarcity produces creativity!

Action Point #6:
Sprint to the Finish Line — The Last Forty Days

The last forty days before my daughter's wedding was when things got really real. The wedding was all we thought about, talked about, and worked towards. In the same way, the last forty days of your MCI are a time for inspiration, full tilt-energy, optimism, attention to detail, marketing, prayer, and trusting God for a miracle. Here are some ideas:

- Forty days of prayer: Involve everyone—kids, youth, and adults. This is a great time to tap into the power of your praying senior adults.

- Six-week teaching series around your MCI: Use the MCI's name as the basis for your series' title. Anchor it in your church's mission, values, vision, and story (Chapters 3 and 4).

- Cast vision. Celebrate wins. Tell stories and connect the dots (Chapter 8).

- Cultivate last-minute ideas. Some of your best ideas will come during this time.

ACTION POINT #7:
MAKE LAUNCH DAY BIG

This is it. The big day. Whether you're relaunching a ministry or the entire church or you're crossing the finish line of some big goal, pull out all the stops to create momentum and celebrate. You might have a big party, a banquet, or some kind of unique celebration. Let the dreams begin!

- Celebrate your Rally Points and High Impact changes.

- Launch new ministries created during your MCI.

- Put a stake in the ground on some new cultural value, such as, "We will be a church who reaches unchurched people."

- Launch a new series.

- Have everyone wearing a shirt with the initiative's name.

- Serve some fun food.

- Get the inflatables out for the kids.

- Brainstorm, brainstorm, brainstorm! Give your best ideas to this day!

Treat Launch Day like a church plant: people praying, signs everywhere, chairs set up, and all-out anticipation. Those who attend will look back and say, "I was there!" This isn't the time to be shy. Invite God to breathe life into your church. On this day, in this moment, at this hour, inspire your church to believe that their best is yet to come!

That's "it," everything you need to recalibrate your church and ignite a fire. Yes, it's going to be a huge amount of work. You will get discouraged. You will get overwhelmed. But your team will be looking to your example. Dig deep and dive deeper into God's grace. You can do this. I believe in you.

> **PRO TIP |**
> Vision narratives (Chapter 3) aren't just for your church. Write out a picture of what your church will look like at the end of your MCI and tape it to your computer. Whenever you want to give less than the full 20%, use it to prod yourself on.

RECALIBRATE NOW

Chapter 12: Walk-through Final Checklist

THINK ABOUT IT!

1. Summarize the big idea of this chapter in your own words.

2. What is something new you learned?

3. What is something you disagree with or don't understand?

TALK ABOUT IT!

1. Why do MCIs make great "silo crashers"?

2. Knowing your own strengths and weaknesses, who do you want on your MCI Relaunch "dream team"?

3. What are some things you can delete, delay, or delegate to focus on your MCI?

4. How are you feeling at this point? Hopeful? Afraid?

TAKE ACTION!

I think you know what's next. You have your Strategy Booklet. You have your MCI Relaunch team. You have your MCI Relaunch Plan. Now just do it! On the following page is a complete checklist.

MCI RELAUNCH PLAN CHECKLIST

☐ Finalize the four essentials of your MCI Relaunch Plan (Chapter 10)

☐ Turn your placeholder date into a concrete date (Chapter 11)

☐ Create a timeline with Mile Markers (Chapter 11)

☐ Build your MCI Relaunch team (Chapter 12)

☐ Make daily progress (Chapter 12)

☐ Schedule accountability meetings (Chapter 12)

☐ Create a financial plan (Chapter 12)

☐ Develop a communication plan (Chapter 12)

☐ Sprint to the finish line (Chapter 12)

☐ Make the Launch Day BIG (Chapter 12)

☐ Set a placeholder date for your next Bolder MCI (Chapter 12)

13

A CULTURE OF CHANGE

"It's about momentum, not metrics."

—Recalibrate Axiom

I'm writing this book in the middle of national and international upheaval. I watched as a novel coronavirus went from international to local news as Washington became the first state to report a case of COVID-19. On March 24, 2020, our governor issued a "stay at home order" in an attempt to slow the pandemic. Church was closed. No gatherings. No pastoral meetings. No Sundays.

No Easter.

Two months later, the news was filled with images of a Minneapolis policeman with his knee pressed into the neck of George Floyd. His death sparked protests throughout our country and across the globe. Some demonstrations spiraled out of control into violence and looting. Less than 30 minutes from my house, the "Capitol Hill Autonomous Zone" attracted national attention.

Just like you, all these events shook me to the core and threw my world upside down. I've been tempted to despair. But at the end of World War II, Winston Churchill said, "Never let a good crisis go to waste." Even as I watched so many churches be driven by fear, I kept saying over and over in my heart, "It's time for the church to recalibrate." This isn't the time to hunker down and just survive. Now is the time to innovate, dream, and rethink the church. This is the greatest time in the last 500 years to recalibrate the church.

One more thing. If you're reading this during the pandemic and still haven't been able to fully reopen your church: when the time comes, don't just reopen—this is the perfect opportunity to relaunch it!

Even without a pandemic, churches face a variety of turning points that force them to change, providing an opportunity to grow stronger or fall apart:

- A church split.
- Moving into a new facility.
- A desperate financial situation.
- Hiring a new pastor.
- A tragedy in the church.

But what about when everything seems to be going fine? Waiting for a pandemic or social turmoil to force you to renovate will lead your church into stagnation. Worse yet, you could drift over the "point of no return" without ever realizing it. It's like waiting for a heart attack before getting in shape. You *can* do that, but you're better off eating healthy and exercising before you're laying in the operating room with your chest open. You must learn to recalibrate without being prompted by a turning point moment. Don't waste a good crisis, but you can renovate without a world pandemic!

Bolder MCI

In Chapter 10, I covered every aspect of the domino diagram except one—the bolder MCI.

Maybe you're thinking, "The last thing I want to think about is another MCI!" But trust me on this: By doing a little bit of work now, you can save yourself more work later. After you've finished your MCI, your church will naturally enter into a season of relative rest. That's okay. MCIs create a wave of momentum and a wave is always followed by a trough. MCI-level effort is not sustainable, but don't rest for too long because that trough is meant to be followed by another wave.

In the process of developing your current MCI, you probably had an MCI worthy idea or two that you had to set aside. That's completely okay. An MCI is meant to be limited in scope—even dating your MCI limits it to a set period of time. Think of that one store in your town that is always having a closeout sale. That just means that it's never having a sale. So, take that Bold Idea you had to set aside and turn it into your next MCI!

Just by having a basic idea of the next moonshot, you can start "greasing the skids" for it during the current one. Maybe you'll be able to set aside a High Impact change or two. Or maybe, you can purchase things now that you'll also use for the next one. And sometimes, the best time to announce your next MCI is at the launch of the current one. You have to be careful about this—ask someone who knows the emotional temperature of your church if they think that another MCI would be exciting or wearying at this time.

Here's the principle I hope you've picked up on: A successful MCI doesn't just accomplish its Rally Points and High Impact changes, but it also creates lasting momentum and a culture of change. The last Recalibrate axiom I want to leave you with is "momentum, not metrics." As long as you create and cultivate momentum, you win.

Even though there are cycles of intensity and rest, there needs to be an overall momentum that's always moving your church towards accomplishing the mission of God. Conversely, if your church isn't in the habit of changing, your people will get used to staying the same and become resistant to change.

At New Life, we've created a culture of change by intentionally making Q1: Rapid Wins all the time—even updating our stage and my "wardrobe" every couple of years—so that the congregation maintains its flexibility. They find strength in our story (Chapter 4) and stability in our Cultural Beams (Chapter 7); yet, they embrace innovation. I'm convinced that this flexibility is what allowed us to not just survive but thrive through the COVID-19 lockdown.

What's more, there's always a shared excitement on my team and in my church for the next big thing. Even as I finish this book, I'm really pumped about the 9.21.21 church relaunch we're organizing. It will be our boldest initiative yet, impacting thousands of souls. Plus, Jana will finally get her new carpet in the sanctuary!

When to Recalibrate

As a consultant, the most frequent question I hear is, "Troy, how often do we need to recalibrate?" I think you know my answer. Leaders never stop recalibrating. One of the guiding principles of successful organizations is "continuous improvement." Leaders develop a sharp eye for things that can be done better, then they make incremental changes. The business world has known this for years. Walt Disney said, "Whenever I go on a ride, I'm always thinking of what's wrong with the thing and how it can be improved."[7] Amazon founder Jeff Bezos said, "It's our job every day to make every important aspect of the customer experience a little bit better."[8] And business expert Tom Peters said, "Excellent firms don't believe in excellence—only in constant improvement and constant change."[9]

It isn't enough to make a half-hearted attempt to renovate, or even to give a full-hearted effort once or twice. Recalibrating is a mindset, not a program. Not a quick fix, but a lifetime commitment to igniting your church, restoring her mission and heartbeat. And the MCI Ignitors is one of the best recalibration tools you have. So instead of asking "How often should I recalibrate?" ask, "How often should I launch a Mission Critical Initiative?"

I like to describe it using computers:

1. Update MCIs: Relaunch a Specific Ministry or System Annually

---

[7] "Walt Disney Quotes," http://www.mywaltdisneyquotes.com/disneyland-quotes/

[8] "5 Time-Tested Success Tips from Amazon Founder Jeff Bezos," John Greathouse, Forbes, April 30, 2013, https://www.forbes.com/sites/johngreathouse/2013/04/30/5-time-tested-success-tips-from-amazon-founder-jeff-bezos/#60488c5b370c

[9] *Thriving on Chaos: Handbook for a Management Revolution*, Thomas J. Peters, cited in LeadershipNOW, https://www.leadershipnow.com/leadershop/9780060971847.html

Whether you're a Mac guy (like me) or a Windows guy (like my editor), you'll occasionally get a notice that it's time to update your operating system. Of course, I get that notice a lot less than my editor since Windows is always needing new virus protection! Anyway, you download the update, your computer restarts, and you get a couple of new features and your computer runs a little better.

I believe you should launch an update-level MCI one to two times a year. Typical update MCI's include:

- Relaunch a Mission Critical Ministry, like kid's ministry.
- Updating your worship or production.
- A significant "spiritual emphasis"—one of my favorite update MCIs was a ninety-day focus on water baptism. It has had an incredible long-term impact on New Life.
- A significant local or international outreach.

2. Upgrade MCIs: Relaunch Your Church Every Three to Five Years

After several years, my computer slows down and can no longer handle the modern demands on its memory. The time I spend waiting for programs to load is worth well more than the cost of upgrading to a new model. In the same way, pastors need to relaunch their churches as a "new model" every three to five years. An upgrade MCI has a sweeping impact on the entire church, restoring its beauty by clarifying its Cultural DNA, retelling its story, and recreating its cultural voice. That's what New Life's 2.12.12 and 3.16.16 MCIs were, and what 9.21.21 will be (yes, we're a little "behind" because of the COVID pandemic).

3. Hard Reset MCIs: Time to Start Over

From time to time, a computer needs a total hard reset—literally wiping the hard drive clean and starting over. Sometimes, a church is so broken that the only way forward is to start all over again. A new name, new bylaws, new everything. Sometimes, a reset is the most courageous decision a leader can make. Here are some ways churches have done a hard reset:

- One church merges with another. A reset allows them to create one new identity.

- A church gives its property to its denomination to be repurposed.

- A pastor transitions to a new ministry or role. A reset allows the new pastor to take ownership.

- Massive societal shifts. The current worldwide pandemic and the racial discussions provide us with perhaps our greatest opportunity for an Upgrade or Hard Reset in the last 500 years.

Now Is the Time

My sincere prayer is that this has been far more than an intellectual exercise for you. I pray that you've seen your own church on every page. That you've found this book at a time when you're ready to lead your church into its best days.

In the story of the Samaritan woman, Jesus tells the disciples that fulfilling God's purpose gave Him sustenance and strength.

> "My food," said Jesus, "is to do the will of him who sent me and to finish his work. Don't you have a saying, 'It's still four months until harvest'? I tell you, open your eyes and look at the fields! They are ripe for harvest.
> (NIV, John 4:34-35)

I believe that Jesus is saying to you, "Don't wait four more months. Recalibrate Now. The harvest is ripe!" Now is the time to ignite a fire in your church. Now is the time to renovate your church. Now is the time to recalibrate your church.

We have a choice: to drift and stagnate, or to trust God to do something special in us and in our churches. Throughout church history, God has used various forces in times of crisis or decline: from the Day of Pentecost to the persecution of the church, from the conversion of Paul to the Council of Jerusalem, from Athanasius to Augustine, from Wesley to Seymour. In each of these seasons, the power of the Holy Spirit inspired leaders to find the courage to recalibrate and move the church forward.

I believe God is calling you to identify the one thing that changes everything, to discover your moonshot, your tipping point, the one domino that will cause a ripple effect in your church. Stop thinking about it. Stop talking about it. Start doing it.

It's your turn, pastor. What's your bold move?

RECALIBRATE NOW

Chapter 13: Select Your Next BOLD Initiative

THINK ABOUT IT!

1. Summarize the big idea of this chapter in your own words.

2. What is something new you learned?

3. What is something you disagree with or don't understand?

TALK ABOUT IT!

1. Do you think that it's important to create a "culture of change"? Why or why not?

2. How can you maintain a solid, time-tested foundation even as you embrace innovation?

3. Is the idea of relaunching your church every three to five years energizing or daunting?

TAKE ACTION!

Set some time aside to loosely map out the next three years of MCIs then create reminders to revisit them with plenty of lead time. The emphasis is on "loosely." You have no idea what may happen next year, but I want you to set yourself up for success by getting them on the calendar now.

One more thing: Be sure to take a break and personally celebrate completing your first MCI!

ABOUT TROY H. JONES

Dr. Troy H. Jones is the Lead Pastor of New Life Church in the Seattle area. Founded in 1926, New Life has grown under his leadership into a multisite church of 5,000 people meeting in five campuses.

Troy holds a doctorate from Assemblies of God Theological Seminary and is a sought-after speaker, coach, and consultant. He is also the founder of The Recalibrate Group and has a passion for helping well-established churches rediscover their vision and excitement.

Troy and Jana, his wife of 32 years, live in a 125-year-old-house that they literally picked up and moved down the street to save from demolition. Their painstaking renovation stands as a testament to their love of old things made new. The pride of their lives is their two daughters, two sons-in-law, and three grandbabies.

Resources

Sometimes you need someone to walk with you alongside you. The Recalibrate Group offers resources at every level to instill hope, provide accountability, and help you implement the principles of *Ignite Your Church* in your own setting.

Recalibrate MasterClass:
Sixteen teachings that go beyond the book, plus a coaching call with Dr. Troy.

Recalibrate Cohorts:
Advance coaching with Dr. Troy and a limited number of other pastors, plus access to a wealth of resources.

Executive Consulting:
Dr. Troy consults the pastor and their team in developing a Mission Critical Initiative, including a self-guided "From the Street to the Seat" 70-point assessment.

For more information or to schedule a free, no obligation initial consultation for executive coaching, visit www.recalibrategroup.com/coaching or email drtroy@recalibrategroup.com.

INVITE TROY TO SPEAK

Looking for a high-energy, no-nonsense, and church-transforming speaker for your next conference or denominational training?

REACH OUT TO US AT

DRTROY@RECALIBRATEGROUP.COM.

ENDORSEMENTS

"Dr. Troy Jones has an easy-to-read style that engages leaders of every-sized church. He is practical, passionate, and focused. You'll find yourself energized as you read this book. Even before he wrote it, I had firsthand experience with these principles through Troy's coaching.

They made a HUGE difference in growth and outreach at my church. And now in my current leadership role with my denomination, I've continued to capitalize on the 'MCI principle.' I am grateful for Troy's influence in my life and know you will be too."

– Dr. Donald E. Ross
Network Leader, Northwest Ministry
Author of *Turnaround Pastor*

"Yes! I've been waiting for this book. For twenty-five years, I've watched Troy love Jesus, invest in pastors, and strengthen the local church. It isn't just Troy's teachings—it's his life.

If you're looking for a practical way to unite your church around the heart of God and ignite mission, I say—read this book and watch what happens."

– Wes Davis
Lead Pastor, newlife.tv

"As his predecessor at New Life Church, I've known Troy since 1989, first up-close as my youth pastor and now at a distance from North Carolina. His ability to think through, and then lead, change is extraordinary.

In his latest book, Troy was able to combine two of his loves—remodeling homes and helping churches. His seven practices can help all of us take the steps to lead our church to the next level. Because he's a practitioner, he breaks down the 'mystery in the methods' to *Ignite Your Church*. Not only does he lead New Life Church and all its campuses, he is actively involved in coaching hundreds of others.

Because of his vast experience, Troy's book gives not just the *how-to* but also the *why*, making it adaptable to every situation. I highly recommend this book to every lead pastor, superintendent, bishop, and overseer."

– Rick Ross
Assemblies of God Superintendent, North Carolina

"Dr. Troy Jones's church leadership acumen is on full display in this book. The principles outlined have the potential to transform the trajectory of your church. It's a game changer! For every pastor interested in taking your church to the next dimension, this book is a must read. Because of Dr. Jones, I have a step-by-step guide for recalibrating the church that I serve, with 100% confidence of a transformative outcome. Thank you, Pastor Jones, for being such a valuable gift the body of Christ."

– Bishop Reggie C. Witherspoon Sr., D.D.
Senior Pastor Mt. Calvary Christian Center Church of God in Christ
Jurisdictional Prelate, Washington Northwest Ecclesiastical Jurisdiction

---

"Dr. Jones offers practical, applicable, principle-based help for the church. His perspective is refreshing as it is offered not from theory, but rather from a true leadership practitioner of church health."

– Rev. Bret L. Allen
Assemblies of God District Superintendent,
Northern California & Nevada District

"This book can transform your church's future and, ultimately, shape heaven.

My wife and I called New Life Church our home for sixteen years and we've had a front-row seat watching the content of this book applied with incredible outcomes. Troy both teaches and lives out these insightful, yet simple, principles. If you're stuck, drifting, considering church multiplication, or know your church can have a greater gospel influence, I highly recommend this book to you."

– Dr. Jeffery Portmann
Church Multiplication Network Director, Assemblies of God, USA

"Dr. Troy Jones is a voice for the local church, not only regionally but globally! His writings and leadership have been an ongoing source of encouragement for me and my staff. It's been said we need *information* to create *inspiration* that culminates in *transformation*.

In his new work, Pastor Troy will take you through all three of these salient steps. Your organization will greatly benefit as you dive into *Ignite Your Church*. Within the first few pages, you'll realize you have a 'winner' on your hands! I wholeheartedly encourage you to put this book into play with your staff and leaders. Whether you're a senior leader or a staff member, your ingenuity will be greatly ignited. After all, you want to be an architect not and arsonist! Give yourself some helpful tools to build the church you'd want to attend!"

– Roger Archer
Founding Pastor, Motion Church

Lightning Source UK Ltd.
Milton Keynes UK
UKHW041831290421
382872UK00009B/376/J